Mirror Mirror by Dianne Wilson

Mirror Mirror Published by Dianne Wilson

Community Version 051616

First published in Australia in 2005

by HarperCollinsPublishers Pty Limited

Copyright © Dianne Wilson 2016

ISBN 978-0-9840387-5-6

Cover Girl: Bella Thomas

Photography: Dominick Alonso

Hairstylist: Ryann Kelly

Cover Graphics: Josh LeGuern

Typeset in Newport Beach, California

Printed in the USA

Author Contact Details:

Dianne Wilson

2727 Campus Dr | Irvine | CA 92612 | USA

Email: dianne.wilson@mirrormirrorgirl.org

To the best of the author's knowledge, facts, statistics and information contained in this book are correct at the time of publishing.

If we have neglected to acknowledge any copyright holders we would appreciate if they could contact the author care of the publishers.

mirror mirror

An Identity Handbook For Life

By Best Selling Author
Dianne Wilson

It all started when I was about 5 years old ...

mirror
mirror

An Identity Handbook For Life

By Best Selling Author
Dianne Wilson

hello future

We all have bad days when we feel like we don't belong - when we feel misunderstood, useless, worthless or unattractive. Now you can say goodbye to those days forever, and discover the real you. Once you discover what stops you feeling positively about yourself, you can grow into the radiant human being you know you're destined to be. So what are you waiting for? Discover the amazing person you were truly born to be... TODAY!

OVER TO YOU!

thank you

Thank you my husband for always treating
me like a queen.
Thank you gorgeous offspring for always
treating me like a majestic mamma.
Thank you Mom and Dad for always
treating me like a princess.
Thank you Father in Heaven for always
treating me like a royal daughter
Thank you for believing in me.

The Imagine Foundation exists to place value on women of all ages and stages of life by empowering them to find freedom from the inside out through developing a healthy self-esteem, valuing their identity, and increasing their resilience.

Dianne Wilson, is the Founding Director of Imagine Foundation, Inc. The foundation was formed as a US 501c3 nonprofit corporation in 2010 with the purpose of using Dianne's experience and resources on the topics of body, soul and spirit, to provide awareness, education, and training in the following focus areas.

Prevention - Imagine Foundation provides tools and training that equip schools and organizations to help equip girls and young women to develop a healthy self-esteem, value their identity, and increase their resilience.

Intervention - Imagine Foundation provides tools and training that equip girls and women who have had an encounter with the justice system, are pregnant, young mothers, or are at risk of or have escaped from domestically violent homes or human trafficking by partnering with organizations that serve at-risk populations including women's shelters, juvenile justice, probation, and corrections department.

Rehabilitation - Imagine Foundation provides tools and training that equip women for their new life outside prison through partnerships with "halfway" transitional homes for women who are ex-prisoners.

Formation - Imagine Foundation provides tools and training that equip women who are incarcerated [many of whom are victims of abuse and violent crimes] form positive values formation while they serve time behind bars through partnerships with jails and prisons.

Globalization - Imagine Foundation provides tools and training that equip women around the world to find freedom in all circumstances through global partners in developing nations and first world nations.

The Mirror Mirror Book and Course is available in several languages and formats adaptable to meet your needs.

The Mirror Mirror Book Club is an informal, intimate format with two or more people who desire to share their journey through the Mirror Mirror Book at their own pace.

The Mirror Mirror Course is a facilitated group discussion led by a trained facilitator following a course outline corresponding to each book chapter. Pace at your discretion or hold a 50-minute session once per week. A facilitator toolkit, training, and assessment tools are available.

The Mirror Mirror Assembly is large group setting where a trained motivational speaker presents one topic of Mirror Mirror. Can be presented as the introduction or launch for a Mirror Mirror Book Club or Course.

Phone: 800.590.3887

Email: more@TheImagineFoundation.com

Website: TheImagineFoundation.com

Follow The Imagine Foundation on social media to receive daily inspirational messages and information on upcoming events.

Facebook: TheImagineFoundationMirrorMirror

Instagram: @theimaginefoundation

truth

"The two most important days in a person's life are the day they are born and the day they find out why.

Mark Twain

who am i?

Discover the Mirror of Truth that reveals your true identity, and a life of true freedom. You were not born to live a small and contained existence, always wishing that life could be different. You were born to live an expansive and fulfilling life. You were born to realize your true value, and you were born to make a difference.

Mirror, Mirror will touch the life of anyone who has ever felt at any time: unattractive, left out, self-conscious, confused, misunderstood, bullied, outcast, abused, useless, worthless or forgotten. This book is full of practical keys to help you unlock the potential of your future. When you know the Truth, the Truth will set you free.

Dianne Wilson

the author

Dianne is a bestselling author [published by both HarperCollins Australia and Random House Australia] and spokesperson on the issues of body, soul, spirit, healthy living, healthy body image, value and identity. Dianne's entrepreneurial approach to life, and her passionate message of freedom have created a platform for her to help many people. Dianne has devoted her life to seeing people live in freedom and released into all that they were created to be. Born and raised in Sydney, Australia, wife of an amazing husband, mother of many gorgeous children, and grandmother too, Dianne is a passionate freedom fighter. Founding Director of the Imagine Foundation, Dianne has a vision to place a copy of her book Mirror Mirror in the hands of every 9th Grade school girl across the USA.

Other Books by Dianne Wilson:

★   Boys, Guys & Men – wisdom for relationships

★   GONE – the moment of surrender

★   It's Time – leadership & character development

★   Body & Soul – a body & soul shaping handbook

★   Here To Eternity – a book of hope in seasons of loss

★   Mirror Mirror – an identity & self-esteem handbook
      [Versions available in: English, Spanish, Vietnamese, Cambodian (Khmer)]

★   Fat Free Forever! – a body shaping handbook

★   Back in Shape After Baby – a body shaping handbook

★   Fat Free Forever Cookbook – a body shaping cookbook

★   Fat Free Forever 101 Tips – a body shaping minibook

★   Easy Exercise for Everybody – a body shaping handbook

Lifestyle Courses by Dianne Wilson:

★   Mirror Mirror – an identity & self-esteem course

★   Body & Soul – a body & soul lifestyle course

contents

Foreword : Dr. Robi & Noleen Sonderegger   15
Introduction : The Mirror of Truth   21

CHAPTER 1   41
Step to Stepping Stone
freedom from dysfunctional family life

CHAPTER 2   61
Celebrate Your Uniqueness
freedom from rejection

CHAPTER 3   79
Your Grass is Always Greener
freedom from body discontentment

CHAPTER 4   99
Under Pressure
freedom from people pleasing

CHAPTER 5   123
The Cyber Social Club
freedom from social media pressure

CHAPTER 6   145
Beware of the Big Bad Wolf
freedom from unhealthy relationships

CHAPTER 7   171

Beneath Skin Deep

freedom from physical and mental challenges

CHAPTER 8   193

The Balancing Act

freedom from eating disorders & extreme behavior

CHAPTER 9   215

Behind Closed Doors

freedom from abuse

CHAPTER 10   237

Stand Tall Princess

freedom from jealousy

CHAPTER 11   263

Pit to Prison to Palace

freedom from discouragement

CHAPTER 12   283

Fully Amazing Grace

freedom from intimidation

Conclusion : A New Perspective   305

Action Plan : Creative Journaling   317

An Expert Opinion   325

Further Reading   329

foreword

Throughout the ages, people have pondered the mystery of life; its meaning and purpose; its trials and its joys. The journey of life is something we experience both alone and with others, never really knowing what is just around the corner. Certainly most of us want the journey to be smooth and peaceful as we seek out our place in this world; yet we know the journey is often fraught with trial and challenge. Whether it be sobriety or addiction; gain or loss; romance or heartbreak; ability or disability; justice or injustice, the ups and downs we all face have the potential to bring us unhinged. To help us negotiate life's triumphs and tragedies, Dianne Wilson extends to the reader some practical down to earth wisdom. With timely insight and from personal experience, Dianne delivers the precious gift of hope. She then signposts the way out of destruction, back into the sunlight of peace. The life-journey she challenges us to take may not be easy, and it may take all the courage we have, but through the careful weaving together of each chapter in this inspired book, Dianne gently shows us that life is worth the risk. Dianne writes with a heart that seeks to let her readers know that no matter what they are facing, they are not alone. Where there is life, there is hope! As you embark upon this journey, may your mind and your heart be renewed in a way that will bring transformation.

Dr. Robi & Noleen Sonderegger
Clinical Psychologists

foreword

Mirror Mirror provides a unique and powerful means of focusing on many of the critical life and death issues people face today, such as insecurity, prejudice, rejection, abuse of all kinds, hatred, jealousy, addictions, social pressure, eating disorders, adoption and family dysfunction. By applying a new twist to some well-known and loved fairy-tales and stories, Dianne Wilson masterfully writes to capture the attention of those most affected by poor or unhealthy self-esteem and consequent destructive behavioral patterns. She confronts the unrealistic and unattainable fantasies and the ugly realities of life. Yet in so doing, she manages to raise genuine hope that true happiness is not just a fairy story, and that no matter what has happened in the past, by addressing critical attitudes and beliefs in the present, the 'happily ever after life' is not an impossible dream. Instead, it is indeed something that can become reality for those courageous enough to continue to dream, to commit and to work to change their current circumstances and belief patterns. Dianne has used some of her own experiences as proof that change and healing are possible, and that each and every person has been created with a divine destiny — if they are prepared to seek it. She has provided relevant information and resources concerning critical issues that can be used effectively for individual personal development, research or in school curriculum and personal development programs. A great book and resource — highly recommended.

Vivienne C Riches

Psychologist

BA, Dip Ed., MA(Hons), PhD, MAPS

Clinical Senior Lecturer, The University of Sydney, Australia

body image

What our eyes see when we look in the mirror.

self-esteem

How we feel about what we see when we look in the mirror; it is our sense of self-worth in relation to the world around us.

be you

Dare to be yourself.

Dream, imagine, explore. Take initiative.

Don't be afraid to face your fears.

Always seek the Truth.

Value your identity.

Celebrate life — take hold of the adventure.

Never settle for less than what you can have and what you can give.

Love never fails so hang onto love with all that you are.

Be strong yet soft.

Spend every moment of your life living — don't waste a moment.

You are royalty with a purpose greater than yourself.

It doesn't matter what life has dealt you — what's happened to you so far.

Your future is in your hands.

Be beautiful — be bold.

Be You!

introduction

The Mirror of Truth

pillars of self-esteem

Value

To think highly of; to hold in high esteem;

to hold in respect and estimation;

to appreciate; to prize.

Worth

Being very highly valued or desirable;

high quality;

deserving of admiration or respect.

Esteem

High estimation or value;

favorable opinion, founded on supposed worth.

Truth

The quality of being true, genuine or factual;

something that is true;

a proven or verified fact; principle.

Hope

To trust or believe;

a feeling or desire for something, usually with

confidence in the possibility of its fulfillment.

Freedom

The state of being free;

liberation from slavery;

the right or privilege of unrestricted access;

the power to order one's own actions and life.

the mirror of truth

A perfect reflection gives you an accurate view.

Body+Soul

Perception is powerful.

What you see is what you believe.

But is what you see who you really are?

Discover the Mirror of Truth.

Find the true you.

Be free.

the emperor's new clothes

Once upon a time, there was an emperor who was obsessed with himself, his appearance and his achievements. The emperor was anxious to become the most popular emperor who ever lived. He wanted to win popularity at any cost.

One day, two shady fashion designers came to the palace, claiming to make the most beautiful line of clothing imaginable.

The emperor was excited about the beautiful clothing, so he sent one of his trusty servants to inspect the designers' work. "Good lord," thought the servant, "I can't see a thing." The unscrupulous designers begged him to step closer to see the quality and workmanship of the special fabric. The poor man stared long and hard but could see nothing. He thought to himself that he must be a fool and, fearing the emperor's volatile response, he left, deciding not to say anything about the invisible fabric. He told the emperor that the clothing was magnificent, so the emperor commissioned a new outfit for the spring royal procession.

The emperor's ever-faithful yet disloyal entourage continued to mutter platitudes such as, "What style! What imagination!" People around the emperor had learned to tell him what he wanted to hear, rather than the truth.

The emperor finally came to see the garments for himself. He stood in shock, as he could see nothing. He said to himself, "Am I a fool, that I cannot see? If I don't wear this outfit, everyone will know that I can't see it. Oh no, nothing could be worse than that! "

Desperately worrying about what people might think, the emperor, in complete denial, said, "The fabric is stupendous. Nothing could be finer!"

The day of the royal procession was drawing near and the emperor was presented with his new clothes. The crooked designers pointed out all the wonderful detail. All the members of the royal court smiled and agreed. Meanwhile, the emperor was secretly feeling like a complete fool, but the need to protect his image consumed him.

Standing in front of the royal mirror, he pretended to look impressed. "A perfect fit!" he said firmly.

Not wanting to be seen as fools themselves, the servants stooped down and pretended to lift the royal cloak from the ground. Everyone went along with it, further fueling the denial in which the emperor was living.

The procession began and the emperor stepped out in his new clothes. Suddenly a voice called out from the crowd, shouting, "He's got nothing on! The emperor is naked!" The people started to whisper and murmur and it wasn't long before the emperor heard what everybody was saying. The emperor blushed deeply, realizing it was true. But pride and fear overtook him, and he insisted that the procession go on. In royal fashion he walked on, completely naked, with his servants holding up his invisible cloak.

Just then, a young boy spoke up above the crowd. "Your Royal Emperor, sir, I thought that I must come and tell you that everyone is laughing at you. Can't you see what's wrong?"

The emperor's heart sank at the boy's honesty. He couldn't hide behind his pretense any longer — there was something compelling about this young boy's honesty that demanded the emperor face the truth. The next day, the royal court cheered with gladness and relief as the emperor had dressed himself for the first time in a long time. In his new-found freedom, the emperor and his subjects were able to live free and happily ever after.

the end

mirror mirror

Mirror, mirror on the wall,
Who's the fairest of them all?
You are, of course!
Why can't you see?
Just be the best that you can be.
Discover the truth inside my frame,
And see your worth and value named.
Hope, truth, grace and freedom bound.
The true you is set at last to be found.

mirror mirror on the wall ...

who is the fairest of them all?

You are, of course! You were not born to live a small and contained life, always wishing that life could be different. You were born to live an expansive and fulfilled life. You were born to make a difference. You were born to know your value, worth and esteem, and to live in truth, hope and freedom, all of which are the foundational pillars of this book. When you live with a correct concept of how truly valuable you are, you will be able to experience the powerful and life-changing dynamic of a positive and healthy identity — body and soul.

Regardless of what life may have dealt you, you are as valuable as the day you were born because your value cannot increase or decrease. Think about a one hundred dollar bill. It was made crisp, fresh, unwrinkled and unstained, not yet used or abused. Then, after a few years of wear and tear, trading and mislaying, it starts to look less pristine than it did the day it was made. Yet regardless of the wear and tear factor, that hundred-dollar bill is still as valuable as the day it was created.

Each one of us was born with our self-esteem intact, and it wasn't until life's blows came along and knocked us around that our self-esteem began to suffer. It is your perspective or opinion that can change and it's my desire that through this book you will see yourself in a new light, discover your true value and begin to esteem yourself in a wonderful new way.

The term *self-esteem* comes from a Greek word meaning reverence for self. *Self* means who we are, body and soul, including the values, beliefs and attitudes that we have about ourselves. *Esteem* means the value and worth that we give something or someone. A healthy self-esteem means that we have a healthy regard for, or opinion of, who we are. This means not considering ourselves more highly or more lowly than we should. A healthy self-esteem is found in the balance.

Self-esteem is an attitude that we have about ourselves, either positive or negative. It is the product of what we see reflected in our mirror under the influence of our culture, society, family and relationships. The development of self-esteem is a dynamic process stemming from two main sources — internal and external. Internal sources involve the way we see ourselves; external factors depend on affirmation from others. Both sources of self-esteem are shaped by internal and external factors and are therefore open to improvement — which is good news!

Henry Ford once said, "If you think you can or you can't, you're right." How true this statement is, because it highlights the power of thinking to shape our lives.

Motivational author Napoleon Hill once said, "A positive mental attitude is an irresistible force that knows no such thing as an immovable body." As we think, so will we be.

Your mirror may be broken, blurred, magnified, compact and inadequate, or you may have put it away so you don't have to face it. This book is designed to be a mirror of truth. It is designed to be a wide-angled lens and to help you to see yourself the way you really are, improve your self-esteem and sense of identity, and show you that you have the potential to live in freedom.

All truth is confronting, but it is truth that brings the conviction necessary for change. When you need to face the truth and make changes, not changing will be destructive to your life. Whatever you fail to change in life you are destined to repeat. At a conference I attended, Dr. A.R. Bernard explained this concept, which I have made into a flow chart for you to follow.

    ↓   Truth

    ↓   Confrontation

    ↓   Courage

    ↓   Decision

    ↓   Dedication

    ↓   Action

    ↓   Change

happily ever after

The journey to truth and freedom, if traveled well, will bring healing and skills to your life so that you will be able to experience:

Happily : joy no matter what
Ever : forever and not temporarily
After : after all you've been through
Life : Heaven on earth.

Remember that settling for good rather than the best is an enemy to your self-esteem. In his book *Self Matters*, Dr. Phillip C McGraw (also known as "Dr. Phil") talks about the influence of society, family, marketers and friends on us to be a certain way. He encourages the true YOU to fight to win every time there is an opportunity for you to feel like you need to become someone else.

It's time to take control of you and your identity! There are many reasons for a person having a poor sense of identity. Whatever the reasons, poor self-esteem results in a distorted view, image or reflection of life. When we grow a healthy self-esteem, we see both ourselves and our world more clearly, and we can live life much more effectively. This book has been written to help you see the truth about you and your identity. The mirror of truth isn't just any ordinary mirror. The mirror of truth is a reflection of what is real rather than just the perception of an ideal.

Objects that reflect or admit light can be looked at in many different ways. A window can either be looked through or looked at, and the same is true of a mirror. Sometimes all we see is the dirt on the window, instead of the expansive view. The same is true of the mirror of truth: you can either look at the shallow smudges on the mirror that detract from your true image, or you can look through the smudges and see the true, deep, clear reflection of who is really there. If you choose to look deep into the mirror of truth, beyond the smudges and the things that you don't like about yourself or your life, you will see and discover many wonderful things about yourself.

It comes down to perception and what you choose to look at and see. You may not be exactly who you want to be right now, but as long as you have breath in your lungs, are grateful for your life, and believe you can get to where you want to be, you are well on your way. You can choose to look into a magnifying glass, which magnifies all your faults and imperfections, or you can look into the mirror of truth, which shows your incredible potential for a life of genuine freedom.

Freedom is not just a final destination; it's a journey. If we don't build healthy self-esteem into our lives when we're young, we will have unhealthy self-esteem and identity issues when we are older. We know that problems don't disappear with age and the reality is that they tend to grow as the years tick along unless we choose to deal with them.

That's why it's not too difficult to find women and men in mid-life going through a crisis that could have been prevented if it had been addressed in earlier years. If we are going to navigate this journey of life successfully, we need to have a proper understanding of our value. Value is not what you do, the title you hold or the way you look. Value is who you are as a person, and you just need to acknowledge and believe it.

Without that real sense of value, healthy self-esteem will always seem elusive. We are more than just our physical bodies – we are both body and soul, and we need to nurture both areas of our lives if we want to have a healthy self-esteem and realize our true identity.

Focusing on just one aspect can cause imbalance in your life, so it's important to remember that there is more to us than what we can see with our eyes:

Physical/body - body image
★ *External*
Emotional/soul - confidence
★ *Internal*

The soul consists of our mind, will and emotions, and it is a key area in determining the outcomes of our life. I like to think of the soul as the steering wheel of life, which can lead us into great health or poor health, great self-esteem or poor self-esteem.

body & soul

Body/External
[physical being/appearance]

★ List what you don't like about your appearance.

★ List what you do like about your appearance.

★ List what you eat in a day on average.

★ List how much exercise you do in a week.

★ Write a plan to improve your eating and exercise habits.

Soul/Internal
[mind/will/emotions]

★ What are your greatest frustrations in life?

★ What thought patterns do you need to change?

★ Challenge the challenges in your life. List what they are.

★ Who do you think understands you best and why?

★ If you could do anything, and you couldn't fail, what would it be?

★ Do you have peace in your heart and mind?

★ List some tragedies that have led to good outcomes.

★ Believe for the best, and for help, when you need guidance or when you face difficult situations.

Just as the body needs nourishment, so does the soul. This can explain why people who are physically well can still find that there is something missing from their lives. In order to help you nurture all of these areas and create balance, I encourage you to start a journal to track your progress.

From this, you can establish how far you have grown during the course of reading this book. At the end of this book, the action plan section includes an outline for a 21-day journal to help you break unhealthy self-esteem cycles that may be present in your life.

Each area of our life affects our identity, either positively or negatively. Regardless of your appearance, job, social class or education, everyone is susceptible to low self-esteem. For some people it may be a constant struggle, shaped by deeply ingrained beliefs with unrealistic relational and social expectations.

Self-esteem, or how well you regard yourself, is important to your wellbeing. People with poor self-esteem usually judge and reject certain aspects of themselves and other people. Sometimes this may be a way of avoiding issues that are too painful to deal with. If you have low self-esteem, you may find it difficult to make friends, go for a job interview or persevere with a long-term goal. Poor self-esteem can often lead to other problems such as eating disorders, depression, alcoholism and substance abuse, child abuse and domestic violence. All of these can come from a feeling of low self-worth. Then there are other traits such as blaming yourself when things go wrong, along with setting standards of perfection that are impossible to attain.

Perhaps you compare your skills and achievements with everyone around you while exaggerating your weaknesses, and you criticize yourself for the smallest and most insignificant mistakes. Maybe you constantly remind yourself of past failures or perhaps you label yourself with words such as stupid, ugly, fat or inadequate. You may even feel that other people are easily bored or ashamed of you. You may also simply lack motivation, be introverted, shy, lacking in confidence and fearful.

I wonder if you've ever met people who suffer from poor self-esteem and observed their behavior? A person may be feeling bad about who they are, their identity may be unstable and they may not be able to feel a sense of self-worth. When people feel like that, there are usually a couple of outcomes. They can either feel terrible about themselves and act like victims, or they can take the opposite track and behave with very challenging, in-your-face behavior. Victims tend to keep quiet, look down, not express their feelings outwardly, procrastinate and often act out their feelings of anger by sabotaging important relationships, while aggressive persecutors put others down so that they can feel better about themselves. These types of people not only have poor self-esteem, but they also have poor coping and communication skills!

If you can relate to any of these traits, your self-esteem could do with a boost. Cheer up — help is on the way! Once you have established that your self-esteem needs improving, the next thing to do is to look at why you feel the way you do. In the following chapters, I have addressed many reasons why our identity suffers and how we can work on improving it. You may see yourself in one or all of the chapters and you may identify with the fairy-tale or story at the beginning of each chapter.

These chapters have been designed to shed light on issues that may have been brushed over or buried deep down in your life. I have personally found through writing this book that I have grown in strength as I have explored the subject of self-esteem and identity and discovered new truths about myself and other people in my life. Truth is a powerful force if used in a positive and constructive way.

I have come to realize more than ever it is our choices that determine the strength and condition of our identity. For every negative, selfish and unhealthy thought or emotion we need to create positive, healthy thoughts and energy, in order to build our identity and build our lives.

unhealthy character

1. Pride

Excessive belief in one's own abilities. It has been called the "sin" from which all others arise. Pride is also known as vanity.

2. Envy

The desire for another person's traits, status, abilities or situation.

3. Gluttony

An inordinate desire to consume more than one requires.

4. Lust

An insatiable craving for the pleasures of the body.

5. Anger

Manifested in the individual who spurns love and opts instead for fury. It is also known as wrath.

6. Greed

The desire for material wealth or gain at any cost, also known as covetousness.

7. Sloth

The avoidance of work, also known as laziness.

healthy character

1. Humility
Freedom from pride and arrogance and a modest (but balanced) estimate of one's own worth.

2. Kindness
The quality of being warm-hearted, considerate, humane, sympathetic, kind and forgiving.

3. Love
A feeling of strong devotion and affection induced by that which delights or commands admiration.

4. Faith
Confident belief in the truth, value or trustworthiness of a person, idea or thing. Belief that does not rest on logical proof or material evidence.

5. Hope
To wish or desire for something with confident expectation, trusting in its fulfillment.

6. Charity
Whatever is given freely to the needy or suffering for their relief; alms; any act of kindness.

7. Grace
The exercise of love, kindness, mercy, favor; a disposition to benefit or serve another.

Life is a process and we're all working through different challenges at different stages, at different times of our lives. Some of these are:

★ Stage 1 : The prisoner or monster within

We need to realize and understand there are things we need to deal with that are holding us back from being all that we were made to be. It's time to get help.

★ Stage 2 : The princess or prince within

We need to realize and understand who we really are and how valuable we really are. See yourself with a crown on your head. It's time to realize.

★ Stage 3 : The wonder woman or super human within

We need to realize and understand that each of our lives has an assignment or purpose attached to it, that we can make life count for something greater than just us. It's time to add the cape to the crown!

Whatever the stage, it's time to face the truth. My version of *The Emperor's New Clothes* at the start of this introduction is a story about self-deception, or denial. Before being able to successfully deal with any issues relating to building healthy self-esteem, facing the facts means that you can no longer live in denial about your problems.

However, facing the facts doesn't mean a life sentence to them. When you determine the truth about what can be changed and what can't, you can move forward into a life of freedom. When we deal with the issues of self that keep us contained, we can begin to build a strong foundation for a healthy identity and we can start to know a life of freedom.

Throughout history, various cultures have used myths, parables and stories to give a sense of identification, value and meaning. I have chosen to retell well-known fairy-tales, stories and parables to help you to identify or see yourself, and to pinpoint the issues that you may need to deal with in order to begin to build a healthy self-esteem.

A parable is described as "the placing of one thing beside another with a view to comparison," or "a narrative drawn from human circumstances; the object of which is to teach a lesson." A parable is basically a short story that uses familiar situations to illustrate a point. The parables here are true to life for all people who struggle to gain a sense of worth and value in terms of their self-esteem.

It's important to remember that in many of the fairy-tales, physical beauty is a metaphor for inner worth. The message is not that beautiful people are better, but that we can all strive for inner beauty, which is made up of virtues such as humility, kindness, love, faith, hope, charity and grace.

I hope you will read between the lines contained in the following chapters and as you do, allow yourself to be changed from within. Each of the chapters begins with a fairy-tale or story which highlights key issues that contribute to or detract from healthy and positive self-esteem.

Some examples of potential issues are listed below:

★   Cinderella: self-pity
★   The Ugly Duckling: self-preservation
★   The Little Mermaid: self-possession
★   Pinocchio: self-absorption
★   Goldilocks: self-destruction
★   Little Red Riding Hood: self-determination
★   Beauty and the Beast: self-consciousness
★   Sleeping Beauty: self-defense
★   Snow White: self-sufficiency
★   Joseph the Dreamer: self-expression
★   The Slave Trader: self-righteousness

Each chapter follows a clear pattern, which will help you apply this book as a life manual to gaining healthy self-esteem and a sense of identity. The outcome of healthier self-esteem is clear, and this is how you will reach your goal:

★   Identify the problem areas in your own life.
★   Be informed about issues you may have to deal with.

★   Acknowledge you are not alone in your problems.

★   Follow the keys to freedom.

★   Continually assess your progress and success.

In my experience in helping people (not to mention as a wife and mother), I have learned a great deal about people and why they feel the way they do about themselves. These great people, full of potential, have inspired me and are my motivation for writing this book.

I trust that these pages and the thoughts and stories that are found within will be like a mirror of truth to you, so you will be able to see yourself the way you really are. I want to encourage you to stop, shine some light, take a good look and see yourself in the mirror of truth, and allow what you see to change your life, from the inside out.

It is my desire to help you honor and value who you and who others really are. As you read, you may experience tears, laughter, anger and pain along the way, but be determined to allow yourself to be challenged and changed.

At the end of each chapter in this book you'll notice that I have created space for you to write your own story, based on your real life experience in the topics discussed within the chapter. I would also love to invite you to share your personal Mirror Mirror freedom stories with us online at mirrormirrorgirl.org!

As you walk out your freedom through practical day-to-day decisions and actions, you will discover healing, breakthrough and improved self-esteem. You will begin to live and love like you've never been hurt – this is true evidence of freedom.

Remember the Truth:
you are worth it!

change for life

I am confident that if you follow the principles contained within the pages of this book, you will be able to see the following changes in your life:

1.   You will be able to accept yourself.

2.   You will not desperately wish you look different.

3.   You will think more about your successes than your failures.

4.   You won't worry about people not liking you.

5.   You will be confident around confident people.

6.   You won't be afraid to take risks.

7.   You will be at ease around attractive and successful people.

8.   You won't be afraid to make mistakes.

9.   You will know your significance and effectiveness.

10.   You will know your true value.

chapter one

Step to Stepping Stone

freedom from dysfunctional family life
[TRUTH breaks the cycle of dysfunction]

cinderella

Once upon a time, a wealthy gentleman lost his beloved wife. Grief-stricken, he remarried, but the woman he chose was very cruel and she hated his lovely daughter, Cinderella. Sadly, soon after Cinderella's father wed this hardhearted woman, he died from a broken heart.

Cinderella's stepmother ordered her to live in the cellar and work with the servants. She felt so small and insignificant; she was unloved and told time and again how useless she was. Cinderella began to lose her identity as her soul became buried beneath the torment of her life.

One day, everyone was invited to a royal ball. Cinderella's two stepsisters made a great fuss of putting on their finest clothes. After they left, Cinderella sat in a corner and wept. Suddenly, Cinderella's godmother arrived and found her precious goddaughter in a terrible state.

"I wish I could go to the ball," sobbed Cinderella.

"You shall," her godmother said, and produced the most magnificent gown, woven in the finest silk and gold, along with a beautiful pair of glass slippers. Cinderella put on the gorgeous gown and slippers and stood nervously in front of the mirror. She couldn't believe her eyes. The mirror reflected her inner beauty, love, kindness, gentleness and self-control. She saw her true self, an image she had not seen for a very long time.

Blooming with newfound confidence, it was Cinderella's turn to be a princess. There was just one condition: she had to return home before midnight, when the magnificent gown would disappear, leaving her in her familiar rags.

When Cinderella arrived at the ball, the prince was immediately drawn to this mysterious young woman and invited her to dance. They danced and danced until suddenly the clock struck twelve. Cinderella fled without even saying goodbye, and in her haste she dropped one of the glass slippers.

When Cinderella arrived home, her godmother was waiting for her. She led Cinderella back to the mirror, but Cinderella was too afraid to look — she couldn't bear to see herself in filthy rags again. When she finally opened her eyes, Cinderella saw that she was as beautiful as she had been just hours before. The mirror had captured her true reflection.

After the ball, the prince could not rest. He proclaimed he would search the kingdom and marry the woman whose foot fit the glass slipper. When his messengers arrived at Cinderella's home the next morning, the stepsisters tried to squeeze their feet into the slipper, but it was impossible for them. Right then, Cinderella knew she had a choice. She could keep her ragged shoes on and remain the servant, or she could dare to step into the glass slipper and into her future.

Trembling, she said, "Sir, please let me try the slipper."

Her stepsisters and stepmother burst out laughing and mocked Cinderella, saying, "This slipper belongs to a princess." But their mockery was soon silenced as the messenger slid the slipper onto her foot and it fit her perfectly. Exchanging her rags for riches, the beautiful young woman held her head high as she walked towards her future with the handsome prince, and they lived together happily ever after.

the end

 fact

Too many marriages end in divorce.

truth

Divorce doesn't have to mean dysfunction.

mirror mirror on the wall ...

why is my family the most dysfunctional of them all?

I am grateful to be an optimist, and I am optimistic enough to believe that we have the power to change our lives, regardless of our circumstances. One of the circumstances affecting today's families and young people more than any other generation in history is the breakdown of the traditional family unit. In a nation and a world where this is escalating, it's important to face the facts about what can be done to help beat the statistics. Living in denial does nothing to help change our present or our future. Once we face the facts, we can then search for the truth and find a solution that will bring freedom to our lives.

Family Breakdown

Today's marriages have a very high chance of ending in divorce. A report issued by the National Marriage Project at Rutgers University said that only 63 percent of American children grow up with both biological parents—the lowest figure in the Western world.

Today we are surrounded by so many people who have experienced divorce that when we come across people who have been married for fifty years, like my parents (who are still madly in love), it's both a pleasant surprise and a rare find.

Any breakdown in marriage affects many more people than just the adults in the marriage. If there are children involved, they are obviously affected, along with other relatives, friends and onlookers. The ripple effect is usually far and wide reaching, and there's often a questioning of one's value and place in life in the midst of any family crisis.

Although these facts represent the lives of many people, they do not necessarily define whether or not a family is functional or dysfunctional. The reality is, functional people make functional families and dysfunctional people make dysfunctional families.

In their book *The Fresh Start Divorce Recovery Workbook,* Bob Burns and Tom Whiteman say, "A family is like a hanging mobile. If one part is moved, all other parts are set in motion as well. They are individual units, but they're tightly connected."

You may have found yourself "in motion" as part of a non-traditional family, but it doesn't mean that you are necessarily part of a non-traditional dysfunctional family. And if there are elements of your family that seem like they don't work or are dysfunctional, you can break the cycle by taking responsibility for and focusing on the truth of your life and making it functional.

Our family should be those who we can rely on, gain security from, and make happy memories with. Sadly, however, because of life's tragedies some have found themselves battling to gain happy and peaceable ground in their family situations. This can destroy, or at the very least disturb, one's sense of personal value and self-esteem. Whether yours is a single parent, step, widowed, foster or seemingly perfect family (no one's really perfect...), I believe you have the ability to rise above your circumstances and become all that you were created to be, regardless of how dysfunctional your family life may be.

Cinderella

Cinderella is a story known to us all. It's the original rags-to-riches, Prince-Charming-to-the-rescue fairy-tale. She was a beautiful young woman, downtrodden by her family dysfunction and the oppression of a cruel stepmother and stepsisters. In order to break the cycle, she had to be brave enough to step out of the mold and to see herself as the beautiful young woman she was, and she had to be willing to begin a new family life. In this instance, her godmother kindly stood her in front of a mirror to show her how truly beautiful she was — inside and out.

Cinderella chose to listen; she chose to listen to her godmother and to believe what she saw in the mirror. This empowered her to ignore the voices of the past: the negativity, criticism, ridicule and all the harsh words of her stepmother and stepsisters. She proved herself able to rise above her circumstances by turning her "stepfamily life" into "stepping stones" to her future.

In a perfect world there wouldn't be marriage break-up and family breakdown, but we are not living in a perfect world. Instead, many of us contend with stepfamily or single parent life, either good or bad. Each of us should be able to enjoy the security that a happy family brings. We should be able to feel safe and secure in who we are as people. Instead, when relationships go through challenges, we can go through feelings of uncertainty, comparisons, jealousy and sibling rivalry. And these are just some of the negative results of a broken home.

In the story, Cinderella faced almost insurmountable obstacles every single day. Instead of complete love and security, Cinderella's life was one of insecurity and obscurity. I can just imagine her crying out in desperation for SPACE from the turmoil!

When our family situation brings a sense of hopelessness, we need to replace it with hopefulness. When we are feeling a sense of worthlessness, we need to take action to produce a sense of being worth something.

When you lose a mother, father, husband, wife, son or daughter, there is a desperate sense of wanting something that you can't have. The tendency is to remain focused on the loss and not on the future. I know what it is to experience the loss of a marriage. All I ever wanted was the "white picket fence" family; after all, that's what I had grown up with and it was all I knew.

Cinderella had lost her mother and became a stepchild, part of a blended family, with a stepmother and stepsisters. She then lost her father and, in his absence, she was subjected to emotional and physical abuse. She was told that she was unattractive and useless.

Cinderella's self-esteem was at an all-time low. She experienced insecurity and uncertainty because she was deprived of the love and concern of a caring family. In her new family she was given no sense of purpose, future or hope. Many people can relate to the story of Cinderella.

When you are told continually that you are worthless, that you don't have value, that you are ugly or stupid and that you will never be good for anything, you will start to believe it, especially when it is your family saying these things. I have lost count of the number of people I've met who have told me about hurtful things family members or people have said to them over and over again and eventually they began to believe what they had been told. The bad stuff is always easier to believe. Negative emotional attacks are soul-destroying, and so too is being completely ignored. It may be that you haven't been consistently insulted, but maybe you are hardly ever noticed, spoken to or considered. Perhaps you feel as though you are so unimportant that no one would notice if you weren't around anymore. That is just not true! That is a lie that has entered your life in order to destroy it. Please believe the truth that you are valuable, important and that you have hope and a future.

The story of Cinderella represents people today who have a number of issues to deal with, both in their family situation and personally, which affects their self-esteem, among other things. We need to find out who we really are and why we were born.

Function vs Dysfunction

You probably know plenty of married people and traditional families that are completely dysfunctional, who live with unhealthy silences, family secrets, infighting and sibling rivalry. One thing is for sure, dysfunction does not discriminate between traditional and blended families.

When it comes to blended family life, I speak from experience. It is something that I have had to come to terms with. In fact, my family now is not considered just blended, it is regarded as "highly blended" because of the complexities of the relationships of some of the people involved. Even so, I am very grateful to be able to say that my immediate family unit is very loving and very functional. In our home there are no *steps*, only people. We choose to put the emphasis on the *father* or the *mother*, the *sister* or the *brother*, not on the step.

I believe we reach a certain age or level of maturity that requires us no longer to blame our parents or ex-spouse for the mess that we may find our family life in. Blame casting only keeps us bound in dysfunction and misery. In order to break the cycle, we need to recognize the dysfunction around us and then take responsibility for our own lives. That's how we discover the truth and break the cycle. Many blended or stepfamilies are anything but dysfunctional. They may have had to work at making it great, but so does any healthy family. I can testify that I have a wonderful, functional (highly blended) family life.

Grief

Stepfamilies exist as a result of some sort of loss. The loss may be the death of a spouse or parent, or the break-up of a marriage or relationship. Adjusting to loss and change is a difficult and complex process, and it involves experiencing grief. Both adults and children grieve.

Adults grieve the loss of a partner and the loss of a marriage or relationship. They also grieve the loss of dreams about the way they thought life would be. They may need to come to terms with the fact that they are not 'the first' for their new partner. Children also grieve.

In his book *Counseling Families After Divorce*, Dr. Gary R. Collins says, "Adolescents live and die by self-esteem. The perception teenagers have of themselves controls virtually every aspect of their development." He then goes on to say, in relation to family breakdown, "Self-esteem losses are strongly influenced by parent absence."

You may be able to relate to the loss of a parent living under the same roof, or even the initial loss of stability at home. Some also suffer the loss or lessened availability of a parent or parents who decide to remarry. There are a number of unsettling issues arising from divorce or death, including a new place to live, new school, loss of friends, having to make new friends, loss of identity, or formation of a new identity or name. There is no doubt that the loss of a person's ideal of family the way they want it to be — greatly affects their sense of self-worth.

The adjustments are enormous when two worlds collide. For most, it's a big adjustment getting married the first time, but for those of us who have been married for the second time, it can be even tougher. The odds are stacked against us and often we have to fight for our marriages and our families in order to maintain a healthy home life.

It's important to realize that it is difficult for some children to adjust. It may be difficult for them to adjust from being the youngest to the middle child, or from being the oldest and most responsible to being the third child down the ladder. They may feel displaced, so maintaining a healthy sense of self-worth can be challenging for them.

Following are some classic comments from children who have gone through family breakdown:

★ "I want my old family back. I miss things the way they were —
even though Mom and Dad fought."

★ "Nobody has enough time for me."

★ "I'm sad when Mom's sad, and I'm sad when Dad's sad, and
they are both sad too much."

★ "I don't know what they want from me."

★ "I'm angry and I don't know why."

★ "Dad is busy with his new family."

★ "It's boring over at Dad's house."

★ "It's great at Dad's house. I wish I could live with Dad."

★ "I miss my father."

★ "Dad and I have a great time, except for her."

★ "He gives more to her kids and to her than us."

★ "He never thought about us when he moved."

★ "Dad left Mom, but he really left me."

★ "There must be something wrong with me."

★ "Mom is wonderful, but that friend of hers is awful. She's always
paying attention to him and not us. She lets him tell us what to
do."

★ "They go away together and leave us alone."

★ "She has always done things for me, and now he says she spoils
me."

★ "She lets him say awful things about me."

★ "I don't want to say hello to him."

★ "I wish he wasn't here."

★ "We've been doing just fine without him. Why do we need him
now?"

★ "I don't know where I belong."

★ "Mom doesn't have enough money. I wish I could help her out."

★ "Dad doesn't know how hard it is at home without him."

★ "My stepmother is NOT my mother, OR the boss in this house!"

★ "It's not fair. . .!"

Myths vs Truth

Seeing the truth about the potential of your own future will enable you
to rise above your family situation. After all, there are myths

surrounding what stepfamily life is like, and it's important to distinguish myths from the truth.

Myth #1: "I love my new partner, so my children will too."

We all know that affection takes time and effort to grow, as not everyone wants to "come on board" and change. Reduce your expectations and you should start to see them exceeded in time. Always respect those around you and watch the changes that will occur.

Myth #2: "Children of divorce and remarriage are damaged forever."

It's true that children go through a painful period of adjustment after a divorce or remarriage. Feelings of guilt overwhelm parents and children as they come to terms with pain. Some feel as though they need to make amends for the rest of their lives. However, the good news is that research indicates that although it takes some time, children can recover emotional stability when issues are addressed. Down the track, they can be found to be no different from children in first marriage families in many significant ways.

Myth #3: "Stepmothers are wicked."

This myth always makes me laugh because I am a stepmother. Stepmothers and stepfathers are often at a disadvantage when they take on their new role because, as research shows, it is the hardest to fulfill in a stepfamily situation. They are often up against resentment, grief and anger, both from their partner's children and from their partner's relatives, colleagues and friends. Be patient and positive, avoid character assassination and let your own light shine through. Change will come over time.

Myth #4: "Adjustment to stepfamily life occurs quickly."

People are optimistic and hopeful when they remarry. They want life to settle down and to get on with being happy. Because stepfamilies can be complicated, it can take years for people to get to know each other, create positive relationships and develop some meaningful family history. Time is a great healer.

Myth #5: "Children adjust to divorce and remarriage more easily if biological fathers (or mothers) withdraw."

The truth is, children will always have two biological parents, and will generally adjust better if they can access both. Sometimes visits can be painful for the non-resident parent, but they are very important to the child's adjustment and emotional health, except in instances of parental abuse or neglect. It helps if the resident parent and stepparent can work towards making access by the non-resident parent an important part of the child's development. This means not viewing the visitations your child has with the non-resident parent as "time out" of your child's life, an inconvenience and not important to the child.

You may be disconnected from your former partner, but the child should never be. They should know that this time is seen as valuable and essential by both parents and it should be meaningful and purposeful. That perhaps means, firstly, changing your attitude and your own schedule. It may also mean sharing things with the other parent that you would rather keep to yourself: photographs, schoolwork, concerts, or sporting events. It may also mean offering to arrange or allowing special outings for your child and former partner to attend, things such as camping, going to the zoo, visiting the museum, having a shopping day, or a day at the beach. You need to value what the other can bring to your child's life and not keep competing. Sometimes this can't happen right away, but it can be something to work towards. Remember, regardless of who's spending the most time with your child or the most money, your child will still love YOU.

Myth #6: "Stepfamilies formed after a parent dies are easier."

People need time to grieve the loss of a loved one, and a remarriage may "reactivate" unfinished grieving. These emotional issues may be played out in the new relationship with detrimental results. It can also be difficult to think realistically about the person who has died. He or she exists in memory, not in reality, and is sometimes elevated to perfection, which makes bonding with the child difficult for the stepparent.

Myth #7: "There is only one kind of family."

This is the myth that says the only kind of family is the biological family. Anything different is said to be dysfunctional. Today there are many different kinds of families: first marriage, single parent, foster and step, to name a few, and each of these present different characteristics and challenges. There are many biological families who live in utter chaos. Dysfunction does not discriminate between biological and blended families and some blended families are very successful. As I have said before, functional families are simply made up of functional people.

Shattered Dreams

Tragically, my white picket fence fell down when my first husband decided that he didn't want to be a family man any more. This meant tragedy for me, and tragedy for our children. In order to get on with our future, we had to learn to focus on the future and not the loss we had experienced. It is absolutely normal and important to grieve when you lose someone either through death or divorce, but eventually you have to change focus to the future. This is not only for your sake, but for your loved ones' sake also.

Our identity is challenged and rocked by going through situations that we don't think we can bear. This kind of experience takes its toll. It is in those situations that we start to compare our life with others and sometimes even question our existence. I have felt like "a nothing" on earth. I can remember feeling like I was living a thrown away existence inside a trash can; a trash can with the lid down tight and a sign on the front saying, "Do not disturb." I was in so much pain that I felt I couldn't bear it. The last thing I would have ever thought at the time was that I was valuable or worth anything at all.

I can remember how incredibly vulnerable I felt when I had to fill out an application form for the first time after my divorce. One set of boxes said "married," "single," "separated," "divorced." When I marked the "divorced" box, I had to make a decision then and there that the mark in the box was not going to frame my life and my future.

New Beginnings

I believe that the happily ever after life of freedom is available to all, regardless of the family situation you may find yourself in. We all need someone to help us see ourselves as we really are. Just as Cinderella stood in front of a mirror and finally saw the truth, we sometimes need a mirror, such as this book, to reflect the truth about our potential, not just the facts about the problems we may be facing.

Problems don't just disappear, they need to be worked through and solved. The key to a life of freedom and a brighter future is to recognize what you cannot change, and learn to live a great life by changing what you can. Many people who have had a traditional family life, only to lose it and begin again, have to face some immense obstacles. In order to conquer these obstacles they can't afford to feel sorry for themselves or take on the woe-is-me-bitter-forever syndrome. The power of forgiveness plays a significant part in the healing and growing process. We have to release the power of forgiveness over our family (yes, those who have caused us grief), in order to move on.

This requires us to forgive them regardless of their response. Forgiving others is the catalyst that sets us free. Forgiving others not only releases others of their debt to us, but it releases us from holding onto resentment or hatred that hurts us and damages our identity. You can make whatever you want of your life if you allow forgiveness and healing to take place. In Chapter 9, you will find some keys on how to forgive others who have hurt you.

Please don't allow labels or any other "boxes" to trap you into a life of containment, a life boxed in your past. You are not defined by your marital, parental or family status. You are defined by who you are as a human being. If I had to rely on marriage for my identity and self-esteem, I would still be living a sad and broken life because my first marriage ended, and I wouldn't be in a healthy state to build another marriage the second time around.

Some of us need the fairy-tale story. Without it, we might believe that life will inevitably be lived in the cellar. We can have the fairy-tale story when we allow the reality in our lives to be overlaid by the happily ever after life story. Have faith for the story to become your reality.

Just as the author of the original Cinderella penned the ending to be happily ever after, you have the opportunity to write your own ending to your life story. It's up to you. I was brought up to believe that I am someone special. You are someone very special too, regardless of whether you are a stepparent or a stepchild. You too can turn the step in your life into stepping-stones to your future. This is not the end of the story. One door may have closed in your life, but you can be sure, as you search, another door will be opened.

Remember the Truth:
divorce doesn't have to mean dysfunction.

beautiful

[beau·ti·ful]

Having beauty; having qualities that give great pleasure or satisfaction to see, hear, think about. Delighting the senses or mind: a beautiful dress; a beautiful speech. Excellent of its kind: wonderful; very pleasing or satisfying. fantastic: extraordinary; incredible.

YOU!

10 keys to freedom

[from dysfunctional family life]

Unlike in fairy-tales, there is no magic wand that you can wave to make change easy. You may find some of these keys enormously challenging, even frightening. It may take time for you to see how they can be applied in your life. Even if they seem too scary or crazy to tackle, give them a try — it's only by breaking out of your box that you can be free. Every positive step you take is one closer to FREEDOM.

1. Resolve to see your life differently and positively from now on and don't be boxed or labeled by words.

2. Don't feel sorry for yourself, as self-pity will keep you trapped.

3. Forgive everyone who has hurt you, and forgive yourself — not always easy, but essential.

4. Be honest and open with how you feel. This means wisely choosing whom you talk to. Find someone who will listen — someone who is mature and will help you move on. Everyone needs someone they can talk to.

5. Try to see the bright side of your life — there is one!

6. Don't dwell on that which you cannot change.

7. Seek professional help if needed.

8. Be patient — building new relationships takes time. Be prepared to wait.

9. Stop thinking about all the things in life you don't have and be grateful for the family, friends, work and home you do have.

10. Believe that you can have a great future, great marriage and great kids, regardless of your past.

body & soul
[action plan]

Body

Your home is your castle, so try to make it as warm and cozy as you possibly can. Looking after your surroundings will help you look after yourself.

Soul

Be a positive contributor to the atmosphere at home. Believe for the family life you desire. Encourage family members whom you may not get along with and they will eventually respond positively. You can make a difference.

**My goal is Freedom
FROM DYSFUNCTIONAL FAMILY LIFE**

my notes
[write your thoughts]

chapter two

Celebrate Your Uniqueness

freedom from rejection
[I cannot always change how people see me,
but I can change how I see me.]

the ugly duckling

Once upon a time, deep in the forest, a mother duck sat on her nest waiting for her eggs to hatch. All but one burst open and the little baby ducklings poked their heads through the shells. The last egg was a large one. The mother duck waited and waited, and became agitated — she was tired of this little duckling even before it was born.

At last, the big egg burst open and the duckling crept out. Not only was he very large and ugly, he sounded different from the others too. The mother duck thought he must have been a turkey because of his size, so she pushed him into the water to see what would happen. Much to her surprise, he swam instantly.

The poor ugly duckling was bitten, pushed and jeered at by the other ducks. Even his brothers and sisters hated him and wished that a cat would pounce on him. He was an outcast. Rejection became part of his life and survival his sole priority. He needed somewhere to belong and someone to belong to.

Seasons changed. The leaves in the forest turned golden and brown and the clouds came in low with heavy snow. It grew cold and the poor little duckling had nowhere to go.

One day he saw a flock of dazzlingly white, graceful swans. He didn't know the name of the beautiful birds, and he didn't know where they were flying to, but he would have loved to join them.

Winter made way for spring and sunshine crept through the reeds. The duckling discovered he could flap his wings. He flew all the way over to a lovely garden.

Out of a thicket came three glorious white swans. The duckling remembered the beautiful creatures, but he felt saddened by their presence. Because of his ugliness he felt he could never be part of their group.

One swan, the leader, was extraordinarily handsome and statuesque; he held himself with grace and authority. The other swans called him the prince. He noticed that the young bird wasn't acting the way he was created to act.

The swan prince flew down towards the young outcast, causing him to bend towards the ground in shame. As the little bird bent down, he saw his own image reflected in a crystal clear pond. He was now a beautiful swan! He saw that he was no longer clumsy, ugly and hateful to look at.

The swan prince's perfection had made the young swan see his own flaws, until he looked into the mirror that reflected the truth of his own beauty and saw his own lovely reflection. The other swans swam around him and stroked him with their beaks. For the first time he was welcomed into a family. For the first time he felt as though he truly belonged.

The sun shone warmly on his wings as they rustled. He lifted his graceful neck and cried happily from the depths of his heart. He had never dreamed of such happiness.

In appreciation for his rescue, the handsome young swan shared his experience with other young swans, encouraging them by telling them that one day they would evolve into the most magnificent of all birds. Together they lived happily ever after.

the end

fact

Everyone faces rejection.

truth

You don't have to live in rejection.

mirror mirror on the wall ...

why do I feel like the biggest reject of them all?

One of the greatest fears faced by people today is the fear of being rejected. It's right up there with the fear of flying, public speaking, spiders and death! At the core of everyone is a desire to be accepted and to belong, and this is natural. Although there is nothing intrinsically wrong with this natural desire, there are times in our lives when it can cause us grief. Each one of us, at some time in our lives, will face the challenge of what to do when we are not accepted by others, and how that makes us feel about ourselves.

We all want to be endorsed, accepted, affirmed, encouraged and welcomed and we all want to belong, but all of us have faced rejection to some degree or other and know the pain that is experienced through being rejected. Rejection is experienced when someone ignores us, puts us aside, declines to be in our presence, excludes us, withholds from us, refuses us, denies or discards us. Rejection is usually expressed in any combination of the following three behaviors: cold and unaffectionate, hostile and aggressive, indifferent and neglecting. When any of these occur, our natural inclination is to shut down, withdraw and escape — internally, externally or both. No one likes being rejected.

Rejection

There are many reasons why people feel rejected, such as:
★ Not fitting in with the crowd
★ Looking different or being different
★ A parent leaving home
★ Relationship breakdown
★ Speech impediment, such as a lisp or stutter
★ Family background
★ Economic status
★ Education (either too much or too little)
★ Race
★ Religion

★ Beliefs, opinion and convictions
★ Disability
★ Shyness and self-consciousness
★ Fear of being rejected

If we look at race for example, America is a melting pot of many different nationalities and cultures, with over 300 million people living in the country. Racial prejudice thirty years ago was much more pronounced than it is today. Fortunately it is now illegal to discriminate against someone based on a person's race or ethnicity. America prides itself on moral values such as respect for difference, tolerance and a common commitment to freedom.

The uniqueness, individuality and that wonderful difference in each one of us is what makes the world, especially America, such a fantastically diverse place to live in. Being born a different shape, size or color should not make any difference, but sadly, often it does.

It's usually a series of circumstances that keeps people trapped by rejection and loneliness. Many are rejected before they are even born. Rejection from birth can be the most difficult to deal with. It can cause people, even those with great potential, to live with that potential unrealized. It's as though they were forced to give up on life before it even started. It's when we finally get a glimpse of who we really are, that we can reject rejection and live our lives above the opinion of others.

All too often, we allow our world to be shaped by other people's opinions. With age, maturity and wisdom, other people's opinions should matter less and less. I can remember times in my earlier years where I felt absolutely crippled by what people thought about me and by not knowing how I could change their opinion of me. I learned that I couldn't change them, but I could change me. I have grown in my own thinking as to who I am and where I belong, so my self-esteem has increased and stabilized, and my identity is secure.

It doesn't seem to matter where we turn, people will always feel free to comment about how we look, what we do and what we believe in. Sometimes we can feel as though we are never going to fit in anywhere. Sometimes people make all kinds of judgments and decide that we're ugly just because we don't look exactly the same as them. What a boring world it would be if we all looked the same. Different isn't ugly, it's just different.

The Ugly Duckling

Growing up, I felt as though I could truly identify with what the little duckling went through (and I really loved the part about him becoming the most beautiful one of them all, as a blossoming swan).

In a perfect world we would all be loved and accepted just the way we are. We would be treated kindly and nurtured to become beautiful, happy and confident people. With this unconditional love and acceptance, we could live in genuine freedom. Our identity would be healthy and we would esteem others because of how we feel about ourselves. Imagine how wonderful it would be if this were true for everyone. It is true for some, but unfortunately it is not a reality for all.

In the story of the ugly duckling, the moment the prince swan extended his unconditional love and acceptance to the young swan, who then caught a glimpse of himself in the mirror of the water, the young swan's eyes were finally opened to see the truth. The truth became his hope. It is only when we experience unconditional love and acceptance that we can catch a glimpse of our true selves, and live free from our pain.

The mirror of who we really are and who we are created to be is available to us, we just need to find it and look into it. Freedom is there for us, but it's up to us to be awakened by the truth. The beautiful young swan could have had negative thoughts when he saw himself as a swan — that he still looked different, or that he still felt like a duck and so spend the rest of his life wishing he was one. But he didn't. The beautiful swan in you is waiting to be awakened and realized. After suffering rejection in his youth, the beautiful swan finally found himself in the midst of a family who loved and accepted him. He finally belonged.

We can all feel awkward and left out, but when we find our rightful place in life, a sense of true belonging overtakes us, making us strong and secure.

The inner beauty of the young swan made him even more attractive and that caused his peers to bow in his presence. He could have lived his life with a chip on his shoulder, saying that the world owed him a favor, but instead he chose to celebrate his newfound existence as the creature he was always destined to be. Being brought up in a family of ducks when you are a swan really isn't the problem; many people are brought up in a family that isn't their biological family through adoption or fostering (see Chapter 1). It was loneliness and the lack of unconditional love that destroyed the young swan's sense of identity — and it was the power of the true reflection he saw in the mirror that brought freedom to his life, forever.

Feeling lonely and alienated from others can be a symptom of low self-esteem. If you consider yourself a bit of a loner and you avoid pursuing or actively engaging in relationships, or if you like working in a job that allows you to work in solitude, not just because you enjoy your own company, but because you are afraid of relationships, then this may be you.

Relationships

The real story is that deep down, most people do crave relationships and can suffer from feelings of deep soul pain because they believe that they don't have the capacity to be accepted.

Many people believe that they will be rejected because it seems as though everyone else wins at relationships except for them. You may have told yourself, over many years in an internal dialogue, that you are inferior to others: not as smart, good looking or capable. You dread being rejected, insulted or put down by others and so you just forgo the desired friendship and companionship to avoid the anticipated pain. You may have even brought rejection upon yourself in order to get the rejection over with. You may doubt that someone could really like you so you test them to prove their affection for you.

On a subconscious level you are saying, "If they really care for me they will still like me even if I provoke them." You may precipitate rejection by saying things you know you shouldn't or by acting foolishly... and then you say to yourself, "You see, I told you I was a loser... everyone else thinks so too. Why am I so lonely... I feel like I am alone against the world. I guess it's my destiny. It's just who I am and what I deserve."

It's very hard to build relationships if you continually anticipate and rehearse rejection. Rejection may start small, as a seed that is planted in our lives through different things that happen to us, but if we don't deal with its negative effects, it will develop roots and it will eventually become a tree with many branches.

If you are rooted in acceptance and love, then you will develop good things in your life like self-control, faithfulness, goodness, kindness, patience, peace, joy and love. If, however, you absorb rejection easily, every rejection will further depress your self-esteem and will reinforce the feelings you may have that you'll never get out of this cycle of loneliness and alienation.

In order to identify rejection in your life, see if you recognize the following characteristics in yourself:

★ Do you have a difficult time loving others and receiving love from others?
★ Are you critical of others?
★ Do you feel inferior or inadequate?
★ Are you an angry person?
★ Are you a perfectionist (arrogance and pride are feelings which try to mask genuine insecurity)?
★ Are you easily hurt?
★ Are you suspicious of others' actions?
★ Do you live your life in isolation to avoid pain?
★ Do you suffer from depression because you failed your own expectations?

The Power of Rejection

The power of rejection is so real that it can cause us to be blind to what is beautiful about ourselves. Sometimes just looking at the people you want to be accepted by can cause immense pain. Also, we can sometimes be unable to walk in acceptance and freedom because we see ourselves as unacceptable.

Not only will others' opinions keep us from being all that we were created to be, our own self-rejecting opinion will keep us in a state of isolation and loneliness. We were never created to be lonely. We were born to be embraced and free, and we need to realize that this true freedom starts from within us. External freedom can't break down an internal prison of fear and low self-esteem, only truly finding oneself can do that.

Living with the pain of rejection is a fact of life for so many people, and this pain is not limited to the young. In cases of complete despair, rejection can cause some people to lose the will to live. Feelings of rejection and isolation have been found to be significant contributing factors in youth suicide in America. It is incredibly tragic that increasing numbers of young people are feeling so desperately unhappy, pressured, rejected and overburdened that they are prepared to take their own lives.

The ratio of male to female suicides is approximately 4:1. The National Institute of Mental Health states that "Four times as many men as women die by suicide; however, women attempt suicide two to three times as often as men."

Although the number of completed suicides is higher for males, the number of attempted suicides is higher for females. Suicide was listed at the eleventh leading cause of death for all ages. There is approximately one suicide for every 25 attempted suicides.

Suicide is a complex issue and although there appears to be no single reason for the increase in youth suicides, a common thread of rejection is found. People today face a combination of pressures and demands that arise in the form of homelessness (family rejection), physical and/or sexual abuse, sexuality, substance abuse, school, family or interpersonal conflicts (relational rejection) or unemployment (job rejection).

The good news is that rejection can be turned around to be a catalyst for positive change. Rejection produces perseverance in some people, and destructive behavior in others. This destructive behavior can include drug-taking and sexual promiscuity to find acceptance and significance, and generally succumbing to negative peer pressure; these things are often a cry for love and attention.

Alienation

I have known the pain of rejection well. I can remember thirty years ago being subjected to racial prejudice because I looked European. I am a fourth-generation Australian, but I have very dark hair and eyes, and in a household and suburb of blonde Australians with blue or green eyes, I continually felt rejected and left out simply because of the way I looked.

In my elementary years I was teased, pushed aside and alienated. I was called names on a daily basis and thought I would never know what it was like to feel accepted and beautiful. My family loved me and told me I was beautiful, but I could only hear loud voices of prejudice booming in my ears telling me how horrible I was. My self-esteem was incredibly low and my identity was uncertain.

It took years and years for me to shake this rejection and I recognize that it always has the potential to return, if I am not very aware of my own sense of identity and security. The key thing that all those years of rejection has done for me is that it has given me grace and understanding for people who also suffer with a sense of rejection. It has become obvious to me over the years that those who inflict pain on others by rejecting them, often themselves have issues of rejection to deal with. Somewhere, sometime, someone rejected them, and now they are projecting that rejection onto others.

The cycle starts with rejection, then self-protection, then projection, and continues on again and again. It's a sad reality that hurt people hurt people (I will be talking more about that in Chapter 12). The fact is, rejection will always come, but you don't need to accept it and you certainly don't need to project it onto others.

Rejecting Rejection

We have all suffered rejection, so it's good to remember that you are not alone. People suffer from rejection for all kinds of reasons, and there are many who have suffered rejection for simply "having a go" in life.

There are lessons to be learned from those whose brilliance often allowed others to reject them and mislabel them as failures. When you think of Walt Disney or Coco Chanel, you don't exactly think of rejection or failure. They are just two of the many famous people who dealt with setbacks and rejection and became brilliant successes. There are so many renowned people with vast personal failures and rejection experiences that it is amazing they managed to succeed at all.

People are often rejected and told they are failures many times before they reach their goal. It is through their determination and self-confidence they prove their critics wrong. The following people have overcome some form of rejection or failure in their lives, to go on to be very successful.

★ **Helen Keller** was the first deaf, mute and blind person to earn a Bachelor of Arts degree. Helen was an amazing American author, political activist and lecturer, despite her health challenges.

★ **JK Rowling**, a single mom and school teacher, had her novel *Harry Potter and the Philosopher's Stone* rejected by numerous publishers. Millions of copies later, those same publishers are probably kicking themselves!

★ **Michael Jordan** was rejected from his high school's basketball team, but went on to become basketball's most celebrated player.

★ **Elle Macpherson,** Australia's most famous supermodel, struggled early on in her career. She often had trouble landing modeling jobs because of her curves, for which she is now world famous.

★ **Coco Chanel**, whose mother passed away when she was 7 and whose father abandoned her soon after, lived with her aunts until she was later sent to an orphanage. When a singing career didn't work out as planned, she grew to be one of the most influential fashion designers in the world.

★ **Beethoven** was physically beaten by his father, and his music teacher said that as a composer, he was hopeless. He went on to become one of the world's greatest ever composers.

★ **Thomas Edison**, the famous inventor, was told as a boy by his teacher that he was too stupid to learn anything. Thomas went on to invent many things, such as the light bulb.

★ **Walt Disney** was fired by a newspaper editor because, he was told, he had no good ideas. Walt didn't give up and went on to build the Disney empire including theme parks, movies and a merchandise empire worth several billion dollars.

★ **Steven Spielberg** dropped out of high school. He was persuaded to come back and placed in a learning-disabled class. He lasted a month and dropped out of school forever, but has become one of the world's most highly acclaimed feature film directors.

★ **Elvis Presley**, who is often referred to as the 'King of Rock n

Roll', was told by the concert hall manager after a performance at Nashville's Grand Ole Opry, that he would be better off returning to Memphis to his former career of driving trucks.

★ **Albert Einstein** was thought to be mentally disabled at school because he took so long to answer questions in class. His grades were so poor that a teacher asked him to quit, saying that he would never amount to anything. Albert Einstein is regarded as one of history's greatest geniuses.

If all these people could turn their rejection into a fantastic future, then I believe that we can too — providing we deal with our negative feelings instead of using them as a stepladder to achievement and success.

In her book *The Root of Rejection*, author Joyce Meyer writes about noted physician and counselor Dr. Tournier's observations on emotional deprivation. He relates the startling fact that a large number of the world's well-known leaders had one thing in common: they were orphans. Some of these super achievers had been victims of abuse and some were severely mistreated. "This is confirmed in numerous studies of high performers," writes Dr. Tournier. He reported that as many as three-quarters of those who become celebrated achievers are estimated to have suffered serious emotional deprivation or hardship in childhood. In extreme cases, because they feel so worthless inside, they work themselves practically to death trying to create some value. As a result of that, many of them become successful.

This kind of approach is unhealthy and unsustainable. That's why we need to work on our hearts and our motives. Our ultimate goal is to be healthy on the inside before we start using our past experiences as a stepladder to our future.

Lesson Learned

Once you have identified the feelings of rejection, you can reject the feelings by refusing them entry into your heart and mind. It's important to recite truthful, positive affirmations about yourself such as "I am highly valuable" and "I am wonderfully made" and begin to accept yourself. It's important that you realize that you are loved. If you don't think anyone loves you, I'm sure there is at least one person out there who loves you; perhaps they have just had difficulty expressing that love to you in a way you can recognize and receive. Your rejection has not been about you, but about other people's inability to accept you as you are, so you can refuse to accept rejection.

I have suffered rejection because of what I believe, and I know I am not alone. It takes courage to stand up for what you believe in, and although I have had people turn their nose up, and misunderstand me at times, I simply won't walk away from my convictions. Because I am a person of conviction, I understand that rejection can sometimes come with the territory because not everyone is going to agree with what I believe.

When we look at how to deal with and benefit from rejection, it is important to realize that it will take confidence to rebuild your life. We also need to take responsibility for our reactions and to realize that rejection is part of learning. Ask yourself the question, "Am I going to let this ruin my life?"

Understanding what is behind someone's rejection of you is a powerful key to the healing process. If you can see clearly that there are issues involved that don't relate to you, it is far easier to reject the rejection coming your way.

Learning from rejection also requires us to look at our own lives to see whether we are doing anything to cause others to reject us. Often we blame other people because they don't want to have anything to do with us, when it actually could be our fault. Many people who live their lives in a hurtful and selfish manner bring rejection and alienation on themselves, and then cry, 'no one loves me.'

I wholeheartedly believe that we should love and accept people and not judge them. However, it would be naive to think that all the behavior of all human beings is acceptable, and that's where it's important to draw the line. We must be accepting of people but learn to decipher and reject those aspects of their lives that cause us pain. You don't have to accept a person's actions, nor do they have to accept yours, but I do believe that we simply need to accept each other as human beings. Our humanity is a great equalizer. This is a vital key to establishing boundaries and learning to reject rejection.

Rejecting rejection is about refusing to take on board another person's negative stereotypes. To do that, one must have a totally integrated, positive identity and acceptance of oneself. We need to understand our incredible value as human beings, regardless of what anyone says, thinks or does against us.

The truth is that your negative feelings about yourself are undeserved and unfair. You may have had some tough setbacks and some ups and downs in relationships so you have convinced yourself in your heart, mind and soul that you are just not a social and likeable person. Begin to say, "I am liked because I am likeable."

List all the things you do like about yourself — body and soul — and work on the things you don't, until your positive list outgrows the negative.

Give yourself time to understand and discover the beauty of your true reflection. Take time to develop the sight of your own eyes, which will see deeper than the eyes of those who do not know or understand. Take the time to find grace for who you are and why you were made.

Remember the Truth:
you don't have to live rejected

10 keys to freedom

[from rejection]

To reject rejection, learn to look clearly at other people's motivations for criticizing and dismissing you. Get an opinion from someone you know and trust. Your FREEDOM will come as you take a stand, tell yourself that you are worth it and then make for the finish line! All of these keys are aimed at building you up rather than letting you be knocked down.

1. Look beyond your faults and see your positive attributes [things you may be good at or like about yourself]. They may not be easy to identify initially, but start with one thing you think might be a positive, or ask a trusted friend.

2. Don't listen to unkind criticism. Choose who you listen to.

3. Choose not to react to other people's prejudiced behavior. This is where it helps to have great friends, or other trusted people we can talk to.

4. Remember that life always has the potential to get better.

5. Enjoy the uniqueness of how you have been created.

6. Work on your internal beauty more than your external beauty. The inward shines further than anything outward!

7. Celebrate the differences in other people. Appreciate them as you would like to be appreciated.

8. The memory of rejection should always help you remember how not to treat others.

9. Don't allow rejection to rock your sense of personal value. You ARE valued!

10. Find out what you were designed and created to achieve with your life, and do it with all of your heart. A little effort will go a long way.

body & soul
[action plan]

Body

Maximize your uniqueness. Be creative with how you present yourself, and make the most of what sets you apart from everyone else. Dress like YOU, talk like YOU, walk like YOU. Create like YOU. Give yourself permission to do this and it will help others in your life to do it too.

Soul

Celebrate your individuality. Research your background and family culture, spend time with like-minded people, and help educate your less-informed friends about your culture and interests. Be thankful for your differences and believe for the ability and wisdom to help others who struggle with alienation and rejection. Use your experience to befriend and include others who feel that they are alone.

**My goal is Freedom
FROM REJECTION**

my notes

[write your thoughts]

chapter three

Your Grass is Always Greener

freedom from body discontent
[One person's faults are another person's fantasy.]

the little mermaid

Once upon a time, a young mermaid lived in a majestic ocean. She was very beautiful; her skin was clear and delicate, her eyes sapphire blue and her body ended in a curvaceous tail. Unlike her sisters who adored the sea, the young mermaid craved freedom from the watery depths.

One day she rose up to the surface of the sea and swam towards the cabin window of a large ship, where she looked inside. She saw a handsome young prince with large dark eyes and the little mermaid instantly fell in love. Suddenly a dreadful storm broke, engulfing the ship with crashing waves. As the ship began to sink, the prince swam through a broken window, deep into the dark sea. The little mermaid swam after him and she held his head above the water and brought him ashore. When a group of humans arrived, the sea-princess quickly swam away.

Longing for a life with the prince, she wished to know everything about the lands above the sea. "Why am I different?" she asked her mother. The little mermaid looked in her large shell mirror and sighed, looking mournfully at her curvaceous tail, wishing she could exchange it for legs so that the prince might fall in love with her.

The next day, on her way back to the surface, she came across a dreadful sea witch. This monster had the power to give her exactly what she wanted, but the cost would be her soul — if the prince married another, the little mermaid would die, her soul claimed by the witch. But not seeing the value of her soul, the mermaid traded it in exchange for the legs and life she thought she wanted.

The spell was cast and the sea delivered her to the shore, but when she met the prince, he did not recognize her. The young woman he loved had a curvaceous tail and lovely personality, but he had not seen her since the night of his rescue. The sea princess now realized the terrible price she had paid for what she thought she really wanted. As the days passed she fell more deeply in love with the prince, yet he saw her only as a friend. His heart belonged elsewhere. He had fallen in love with the little mermaid as she was. He no longer recognized her.

Soon it was announced that the prince must marry, and that the daughter of a neighboring king would be his wife. The little mermaid felt as if her heart was breaking in two. She thought her human form would cause the prince to love her more, but alas, he didn't even recognize her now.

The wedding ceremony began and the little mermaid heard noises behind the rocks on the shore. It was her sisters, who had come to rescue her. "Quickly!" they said. "Come with us! If you come back to the sea before the prince marries, your life will be saved. We gave our precious jewels to the sea monster in exchange for your life." The little mermaid was rescued just in time.

The little mermaid returned to the sea and her family. She looked into her shell mirror once again and now saw her true magnificence. She was grateful for a second chance under the sea, where she belonged. And the little mermaid lived a contented life happily ever after.

the end

fact

Most people are discontent with their body.

truth

Contentment starts from within.

mirror mirror on the wall ...

why don't I like what I see at all?

If you can relate to this question, you're not alone. Thousands of women and an increasing number of men look in the mirror every day and dislike or even despise what they see.

When you look in the mirror, what do you see? When you walk past a store window and catch a glimpse of your body, what do you notice first? Do you see something you like, something you are proud of, something you were born with and live with happily? Or do you criticize and pick apart how you look in your mind: I'm too fat, I'm too puny, my breasts aren't the right size, I'm too short? And if this is the case, do you wonder why you think this? What about your naked body in front of a mirror — do you avoid mirrors when having a shower?

However, one person's faults are another person's fantasy. Sometimes we get caught up on facts, like our feet being too wide or our nose being too big or our lips being too thin and our hips too full, when we should be looking at the truth, which says that we are all beautiful in our own way.

Sometimes we are simply never satisfied with what we have and how we have been made, and we are too busy focusing on all of our faults instead of celebrating or appreciating our strengths. My personal observation has shown me that it doesn't matter how beautiful someone is, there's always something about the way they look or sound that they don't like.

One thing is certain: for every body part you are dissatisfied with, there will be another person wanting to swap with you!

In a world that judges men and women alike on the way they look, it's important to discover for yourself what your life priorities are. Brawn, brains and beauty may be an attractive combination, but vanity is not. Are your looks more important to you than your character, or is your character all that matters so you neglect your looks? How about a balance of both? Living a balanced life opens you up to great opportunities and a life of freedom.

Body Discontentment

Let's take a look at some examples of certain aspects of our bodies that we sometimes wish we could change. See if you can identify with any one or more of these:

★ Height
★ Weight
★ Hair
★ Eyes
★ Skin
★ Body type
★ Facial features
★ Bone structure
★ Voice

The list could go on! While understanding that what we think is beautiful may actually be different through someone else's eyes, it is also important for us to appreciate different kinds of beauty that may not necessarily be to our taste. We need to appreciate what we have and the life we've been given.

Following are some facts and figures relating to body image dissatisfaction:

★ Adolescent girls are consistently more dissatisfied with their bodies than adolescent boys. In a survey of high school students, 70 percent of adolescent girls wanted to be thinner, compared to 34 percent of boys. Only 7 percent of girls reported wanting to be larger, in comparison to 35 percent of the boys surveyed.

★ A study involving 869 girls aged fourteen to sixteen found that more than one-third (36 percent) of the girls reported using at least one extreme dieting method in the past month (crash dieting, fasting, slimming tablets, diuretics, laxatives or cigarettes). In addition, 77 percent of the girls said they wanted to lose weight.

One way to measure how you feel about different aspects of yourself is by scoring each on a scale from one to ten, one being complete contentment and ten being extreme discontentment. I suggest that anything over the five line means you have some work to do. Then you need to determine which of those things scored over five you can actually change for the better, and those you can't. If it's something like being under or overweight, and you know you can do something to improve, then that's what you need to focus on until you can give it a lower score than five. If it's something like your height, then you just need to acknowledge you can't change that, so be thankful for how you are made and look for all the positive things that come with being either short or tall. For example, if you are shorter than most people, you will have no trouble finding pants long enough to fit you, even if you do have to get everything taken up! On the other hand, taller people have no trouble reaching the top shelves at the supermarket, or seeing above a crowd.

The Little Mermaid

The grass always looks greener on the other side of the fence. In my version of the classic fairy-tale *The Little Mermaid*, a story is told of someone wanting something that they didn't have. And in this case, it was a ten out of ten for dissatisfaction to the point where she was prepared to sell her soul to get what she wanted.

There's a whole future life waiting for us when we get comfortable with who we really are and how we are made. If you were born with curves, be grateful for them, because they are truly beautiful. If however, you were born petite, be grateful for that, because you are also truly beautiful.

There is true beauty in every body shape, whether big or small, curvy or petite. The little mermaid lived a life of discontentment, always wishing she was someone else. She aspired to the unobtainable, didn't appreciate what she had, and was prepared to sell her soul in order to gain what she wasn't born with. Her life became full of fear and pain as she sacrificed who she really was to become someone else, someone she was never meant to be. Her whole focus was unhealthy.

Although we sometimes wish to be able to enter the world of another whose life seems much better than ours because of how they look versus how we look, in reality our lives contain the same expansive potential if we just choose to maximize what we have.

Many people today struggle with gross dissatisfaction in how they look and they live in a permanent state of wanting what they don't have. We refuse to listen to other people's affirmation of our beauty, we idolize what is unattainable, and we keep dreaming that the grass is greener on the other side of the fence.

Body Image

Most people think of body image as the picture of the body in the mind's eye. This is only one of four factors that determine our final body image. Body image is the sum total of the visual, emotional, physical and historical aspects of a person and is influenced by their own beliefs and attitudes as well as ideals in society.

In their book *Unloading the Overload*, Dr. Cliff Powell and Dr. Graham Barker say, "Self-image is the internal view we have of ourselves, the permanent picture we see inside that dictates most of our actions and responses."

We will always have some sort of self-image or body image, but that image does not remain the same. Instead, it changes in response to events throughout our life, such as puberty, pregnancy, disability, illness, surgery, menopause, and even different stages in a woman's menstrual cycle. Body image is closely connected to a person's self-esteem. Self-esteem refers to how much a person values or accepts themselves for who and what they are.

We live in a culture that worships thinness. Images of women in the media, advertising and popular culture emphasize beauty, youth and being thin. As some of us don't score highly in one or more of these categories, our body image is often poor. Advertisers speak of 'perfect bodies,' suggesting that body flaws should be hidden or even surgically corrected. The diet, exercise, cosmetic surgery and beauty industries are making obscene amounts of money from people's body image misery as we pursue the seemingly ideal body and look.

The problem with the promotion of this kind of ideal is that it does not empower us, rather it undermines our confidence in who we are and how we are made. We do not need to measure up to someone else's idea in order to be truly beautiful and valued. Not liking something is considered normal human nature; having a 'complex' about yourself, however, will keep you from living free.

There are many things that we may not particularly like about ourselves, but there's a big difference between not liking and outright discontentment, which this chapter is about.

There are also many things that take part in shaping the feelings we have about our bodies. Following is a look at some common factors.

★ *Media*: social media, television, movies, magazines and other media sources give out messages about what the ideal body looks like.

★ *Family members*: how those closest to us feel about their bodies usually affects the development of our own body image.

★ *Abuse*: sexual, emotional and physical abuse has a negative impact on body image.

★ *Diet fads*: unhealthy eating and exercise can cause not only physical damage but also emotional damage, affecting our self-esteem.

★ *Emotional experiences*: both positive praise and negative criticism received during childhood and adulthood can affect our self-esteem.

★ *Perfectionism*: an unrealistic desire to be better, fitter, thinner, bigger, prettier or curvier will always end in disappointment.

★ *Our partners*: the way we are treated by our significant others plays a part in the way we see ourselves. We tend to absorb criticism from those we love.

Body image affects more than our behavior, it also influences our self-esteem and our identity. Studies indicate that, regardless of actual attractiveness, the better a person feels about his or her body, the higher his or her self-esteem, and vice versa.

It is hard to not be affected by the media bombarding us constantly with the message "thin is in!" On TV commercials we are told to "lose weight fast" or "exercise for five minutes a day" to have a beautiful body; magazines display thin, attractive women to try to convince us that we are not acceptable until we have slim, toned thighs. The overriding message is that we need to change something about ourselves in order to be loved or successful. In particular, if we have thin, fit bodies, we are led to believe that our lives will be perfect.

My experience has demonstrated that this message is not true. In fact, the constant striving to be something other than what we are is part of what can keep us dissatisfied with life. The reality is that genetically, we are all born with varying shapes and sizes. A very small percentage of the world's population can expect to achieve the shapes and sizes the media portrays as ideal without endangering their health or resorting to surgery. The media holds this unrealistic goal up to us and suggests we try to reach it. No wonder so many men and women are struggling with body image dissatisfaction.

The role of body image in the development of eating disorders in adolescent girls is fairly well documented. It is also known that parents have a powerful influence over their children's eating habits. One study found that 40 percent of 9 and 10 year old girls trying to lose weight generally did so with the influence of their mothers.

There is increasing evidence that boys too are subjected to pressure to attain the "perfect" body. In extreme cases, this may lead them to use muscle-building steroids.

Model and actress Cameron Diaz, when asked about her body in a magazine interview, replied, "I'm 5 foot 9 inches, weigh 120 pounds and I wear a size four. I'm comfortable with my body. I love it... I think I have a nice body, I'm happy with it."

That's great for Cameron, but what about us! Are you comfortable with your body? Could you honestly say you love it?

Distortion and Dissatisfaction

There are two general types of body image disturbances: distortion and dissatisfaction.

Body image distortion is exactly like the person looking at a wide, narrow, short or tall mirror at a carnival, and it is characterized by an inaccurate or distorted visual image of the body. Thin people who see themselves as fat experience a body image distortion. Some of them truly believe they are fat and are unable to challenge this thinking. Others can see themselves as thin when looking in a mirror, but nevertheless feel fat.

People struggling with anorexia nervosa experience a body image distortion and as a result, starve themselves. Re-feeding the body and retraining the mind are both necessary parts of the treatment for this type of body image distortion.

Body dissatisfaction occurs when a person feels negatively towards his or her body or towards specific parts of his or her body.

There are two components to body dissatisfaction: displeasure with the way you see your body in your own mind, and discontentment with the way you feel about your bodily appearance. This dissatisfaction can be felt in varying degrees. Some people experience mild feelings of unattractiveness, while others become obsessed with the way they look, which hinders them dramatically from functioning as a normal human being.

Body image dissatisfaction is so prevalent in our society that it has almost been classified as normal, particularly among teenagers and young adults, both female and male with little distinction between socio-economic group or ethnicity. So much emphasis has been put on the plight of individual teenage girls battling their own distorted body image that the whole picture is rarely seen. The whole picture is that it affects every one of us.

It seems that some of the most gorgeous models and actresses, who have been voted as having the best bodies in the business, still find reason to complain about certain body parts. Often those women whose body shape is curvy want to be skinny and those who are skinny want more curves. People with darker skin are trying to be fairer and those with fairer skin are sun bathing in order to get darker!

Thin lips, fat lips, blonde hair, dark hair, hippy, curvy, thin, busty — the list goes on. Some people can't stand to see photographs or video footage of themselves, or listen to the sound of their voice on tape. There always seems to be something to be unhappy about.

People seem to want what they don't have. Will we ever be happy? The extent of the dissatisfaction determines the impact it has on a person's life. For example, many people with eating disorders hate their bodies so much they wish they were invisible — many hide in baggy clothes. Some are unable to tolerate loving or affectionate touch and others retreat from social interactions. Many people can be so affected by their dissatisfaction that they choose not to participate in activities that involve wearing revealing attire such as bathing suits or fitted clothes.

When it comes to body dissatisfaction, picture Michael Jackson and the distortion of his appearance, stemming from his desire to look like someone else. His face was transformed into a different shape and color and he didn't even resemble the nice-looking young man he once was. He was the same person inside, however, and no amount of exterior change ever altered that fact.

We don't need to strive to be something or someone we are not.

We each have a personal best to aim towards and it's when we reach our personal best that we are *teleios*, which is an ancient Greek word meaning perfect for now, that is, perfect at one's own particular stage of development.

You can choose either to be on a quest for the ideal of perfection, which is the never happily ever after life, or learn to live in appreciation of who you are.

Beautiful Hollywood actress Jennifer Aniston believes she has "a big butt." In a magazine article Jennifer was quoted as saying, "I'm not comfortable being heavy. Whenever I gain weight, it goes to my rear." Jennifer also commented that she wished she had longer legs and not such big hips. If only she could truly see herself!

Change

If you need to change the essence of who you are so someone will accept you, that is wrong. Chasing someone else's looks, life and existence will only rob you of your own. It is not wrong, however, to dream of a better life or even a different life, but to change the essence of you is not the right way to go about it.

Just remember, you can do whatever you want and change whatever you want, but you can't choose the consequences of your choices, or change them later.

You are body and soul, so changing the way you look doesn't mean you're changing who you really are. You can't escape you!

Having said that, there is nothing wrong at all with wanting to improve yourself; in fact, that's desirable. Wanting to improve what you have does not equal being discontent. Being discontent with unhealthy aspects of your life is a very positive thing, but just remember, trying to be like someone else will only ever make you a poor imitation of the real thing.

Some people simply don't like themselves and they question the reason for their existence because of their poor self-esteem, poor body image and circumstances in life.

"Why was I born?" many have sadly asked.

If you have ever asked that question, I want to encourage you to see your life differently. Instead of asking why you were born, how about asking, "Why is there breath in my lungs today?" Could it be that you have an incredible purpose and opportunity in your day — in your life?

Questioning your existence implies that you feel there is no purpose or reason for living. On the other hand, asking yourself what opportunities may be in front of you implies that there is a purpose and destiny that you need to fulfill. Changing your perspective will help change your life.

The process of changing your perspective doesn't start with your body, it needs to start with your mind. Change your mind, change your life! Addressing these issues will open a door, beyond which you can start to develop a fondness towards yourself that will see you on your way to improved contentment about who you are and how you are made.

Try the following positive steps to counteract any unhelpful thoughts you've had about yourself:

★ Do not criticize yourself publicly or privately.
★ Do not punish yourself emotionally or physically.
★ Be patient and kind to yourself.
★ Celebrate other people's beauty and success.
★ Look in the mirror and smile at your beauty.
★ Allow others to encourage you
★ Believe you were born on the "A" team.
★ Believe you are valuable no matter how you look.
★ Always stand tall in a room full of beautiful people.
★ Be glad you are YOU.

To actively pursue these positive thoughts and a healthier body image, we need to resist any stereotypical attitudes in us or in others that say that only thin is beautiful. If there is any obsession in your life about how much you weigh, it's time to throw out your scales, as your worth cannot be measured by your weight! Ignore the unhealthy message that the media try to bombard you with. Remember, they are just trying to sell you something.

It's important to be healthy but not obsessive with food, as food is not your enemy or your ally, it's simply fuel to live and to be enjoyed. Also, for every negative thought you have about yourself, find a positive counterpart; if you can't think of anything great to say about yourself, don't say anything at all.

Sometimes we can find it difficult to accept encouraging comments given by others. A free and confident person is able to accept encouragement, but also knows to reject flattery. The difference between encouragement and flattery has to do with the motive with which the comments are made. An "encourager" in your life will only use truth to build you up, however a "flatterer" will use whatever is needed (it could be a truth, or a lie) for selfish means, to get what they want from you. Accepting what you can't change and setting a range of short and long-term goals to change what you can (without compromising who you are), is an important part of the process. Write yourself a list of areas of your life that you want to improve that are beyond your looks. Also, get out and take a positive look at other people. This will help to grow your worldview and help you see that people of all different shapes and sizes are beautiful, including you.

Be Content

I have learned to be content, even though it is human to want something that I don't have. I have straight hair and I wish it were curly like one of my friends, Jules. Jules, on the other hand, doesn't like her hair so she prefers it tied back or straightened. I'm also very tall, nearly 5 foot 9 inches, and for a woman, that's both good and bad. Good for a modeling career, bad for a long haul flight to Europe or New York, and not so great if you're not into basketball-type guys!

When I began modeling in my late teenage years, I had to learn to be grateful for my body shape and I also had to be prepared to work on aspects that needed improvement. I am curvy and so I was given work that required me to be that way. I was not asked to go to castings as a skinny editorial model because that is not me, and no amount of dieting would help me lose my bone structure. I was able to portray good health and good self-esteem in a sometimes unhealthy environment.

This doesn't mean, however, that I was exempt from criticism. Once I missed out on work because of "faults" with my looks — I missed a big advertising campaign simply because of a freckle beneath my bottom lip. It was just as easy for the company to book a dark-haired model with no freckle and so that's exactly what they did, and I don't despise my freckle because of what happened.

During my years as a model, the amazing thing was that I got many jobs because of aspects of my body that I had previously not liked and wished I could change. Although it didn't necessarily make me feel better about myself on the inside (again — human nature), I did come to realize that beauty really is in the eye of the beholder.

Acceptance

Be informed, consider the facts and accept the truth, so that you can begin to live in contentment. Here is some information a friend sent me that I think was quite insightful:

★ There are three billion women who don't look like supermodels and only a few who do.

★ Marilyn Monroe wore a size fourteen.

★ If Barbie were a real woman, she'd have to walk on all fours due to her proportions.

★ The average American woman weighs 165 pounds and wears size fourteen.

★ One out of every four 18 to 25-year-old women has an eating disorder.

★ The models in the magazines are airbrushed and not perfect!

★ A psychological study in 1995 found that three minutes spent looking at a fashion magazine caused 70 percent of women to feel depressed, guilty and ashamed.

★ Models twenty years ago weighed 8 percent less than the average woman. Today they weigh 23 percent less than the average woman.

If you feel as though you've tried everything and nothing seems to be working for you, it may be necessary for you to seek professional help. Sometimes someone else leading us towards the mirror of truth is what we need to be set free.

In his book *The Balance of Beauty,* fashion industry hair and makeup artist Gregory Landsman writes, "The belief in equality of beauty allows us to know that no one is better than who we are, but in the same breath, no one is less. In recognizing this truth we can regain the essence of beauty with which we were born."

In order for you to live a life of true freedom from body discontentment, you need not only to understand how lovely you are inside and out, but you need a deep revelation that won't be shaken — no matter what criticism comes your way. My hope for you is that this deep revelation will make its way permanently into your heart and mind, so you can live in freedom.

Remember the Truth:
contentment starts from within.

10 keys to freedom
[from body discontentment]

Body contentment will never be achieved through knowing how you *should* look; it's about appreciating how you are *now*, so you can make healthy changes. FREEDOM is just a thought away!

1. Be grateful for how you were made: no compromise.

2. Take care of yourself and improve what you have.

3. Accept encouragement and discourage flattery.

4. Look in the mirror every day and tell yourself you are beautiful and intelligent.

5. Stop looking at other people and wishing you were them.

6. Stop allowing social media to determine beauty in your eyes.

7. Encourage someone every day about their value and beauty.

8. Don't chase and strive for what doesn't belong in your life.

9. Choose only the best for your life.

10. Recognize your natural body shape (naturally thin, athletic or curvy) and be content to be the best you can be, with the body shape you were born with.

body & soul
[action plan]

Body

Showcase your best assets (modestly of course!), and work with problem areas by savvy dressing and perhaps choosing darker colors where you don't want to be noticed.

Soul

Continually remind yourself that you are beautiful, that nobody is perfect and that you have the right to feel fantastic about yourself. Seek help to do whatever you need to do to feel better about yourself, whether it's losing weight, gaining weight, or simply accepting yourself just the way you are.

**My goal is Freedom
FROM BODY DISCONTENTMENT**

my notes

[write your thoughts]

chapter four

Under Pressure

freedom from people pleasing
["We spend more, but have less ... we have
multiplied our possessions but reduced our values ..."]

pinocchio

Once upon a time, a cobbler named Geppetto who had always wanted a son decided to make himself a little puppet. Geppetto hid a kind heart inside the puppet and named him Pinocchio. He designed the boy to move by the strings attached to him, but in the wrong hands these strings could lead the boy astray.

Having sold some precious items in order to buy Pinocchio's first schoolbook, Geppetto sent the overjoyed puppet off for his first day at school. On the way, Pinocchio saw a traveling circus and was stopped by one of the performers. Feeling pressured, he sold his schoolbook for entry to the circus. Pinocchio was completely caught up in the crowd; he decided then and there that he wanted to be famous like the circus performers.

The circus manager saw Pinocchio and, thinking he could make some money out of him, put him on show in a cage. Pinocchio cried and begged to be released from the cage, until eventually, the circus manager let him go. He was free at last, and he set out for home without delay.

A beautiful angel, seeing Pinocchio running home, swooped down to ask if he was okay.

"Tell me what has happened," she said. Pinocchio told her his story, leaving out the part about selling his first reading book. Suddenly, Pinocchio's nose began to grow longer. "You're not telling the truth, are you?" asked the angel. Blushing with shame, Pinocchio began to weep. Because she felt sorry for him, the angel clapped her hands and his nose shrank to its proper length.

"Now, don't tell any more lies," the angel warned him. "Go home right away to your father."

Grateful, he ran towards home. On the way home, Pinocchio came across Carlo, the lazybones of his class. "Why don't you come to Toyland with me?" said Carlo. "You can stay as long as you want to and play all day long!" Ignoring his promises to the angel and his conscience, Pinocchio agreed to go. Pinocchio wanted to be just like Carlo — he copied everything Carlo did, hoping Carlo would be his friend. So off they went to Toyland. "This is the life!" he said to Carlo nervously, hoping that everything would be okay.

Pinocchio and Carlo had been at Toyland a number of days when they awoke to a terrible surprise. They had each sprouted a long pair of hairy donkey ears! The boys had become just like donkeys and were taken swiftly by the Toyland owner to the market to be sold.

Separated from his so-called friend, Pinocchio was sold to a farmer who beat him every day. Desperate for help, Pinocchio called out for the angel.

The angel heard Pinocchio's call and saved him, turning him back into a wooden puppet. Then she helped him find his way home. Pinocchio finally realized that following the crowd was only going to harm him and he decided to be honest with himself and his father. This time Pinocchio's heart was genuine and when he looked in the mirror the next morning, he had become a real boy.

Pinocchio went on to become a great leader instead of a weak follower, having learned lessons from his mistakes. Pinocchio no longer lived like a puppet on string, and lived happily ever after.

the end

Fact

Everyone faces peer pressure.

truth

Confidence allows you to live with "no strings attached."

mirror mirror on the wall ...

why is there so much pressure to conform?

What possesses a person to follow another person blindly through life? I believe the answer to this question lies within a person's self-esteem and values. Once we understand who we are and why we were made, we can determine what it is that we are meant to do.

Peer pressure is the most common and often the most powerful tool of conformity. It usually starts at school when friends encourage us to become just like them and to do as they do. This same pressure then continues through to adulthood if we don't take a stand and decide for ourselves who we are meant to be and what we are meant to do.

All of us begin in life like blocks of wood or pieces of clay, and we need shaping and molding to help us grow and mature. Fighting the shaping process will only keep you in the workshop or on the potter's wheel of life for longer. We can enable that shaping or molding process by letting people who have experience in life and who are positive role models help us negotiate the twists, turns and challenges of life. Our tendency is always to think we know better. But people who are living positive lives have already done the hard yards and we can learn from them. Parents can be a great example of this.

When I was seventeen I thought I knew everything, that was until I got married and had kids of my own! Often people can't seem to see or appreciate what they have until they grow up and see for themselves what a great job their parents have actually done. Our human nature tends to always want to know everything and to always be right, even when we may know very little, and are frequently wrong and led away from the truth.

Peer Pressure

Peer pressure means that friends or acquaintances compel you to do something you may not want to do. They may urge you through negative peer pressure to cheat, steal or say something to someone that you feel uncomfortable about. People who conform to peer pressure are often called 'people pleasers.'

In her book *The Disease to Please*, Dr. Harriet Braiker says, "People pleasers are not just nice people who go overboard trying to make everyone happy. Those who suffer from the 'Disease to Please' are people who say 'Yes' when they really want to say 'No' — but they can't. They feel the uncontrollable need for the elusive approval of others like an addictive pull. Their debilitating fears of anger and confrontation force them to use 'niceness' and 'people pleasing' as self-defense camouflage."

Peer pressure is not always a negative force. Powerful, positive peer pressure can shape positive behavior in people. For example, in some schools with bullying problems, peer pressure has been used to influence bullies to reverse their behavior. In many elementary schools, peer groups have joined together to prevent bullying.

Some people give in to negative peer pressure and people pleasing because they want to be liked, to fit in, or because they worry that others may make fun of them if they don't go along with what other people want. Others may conform because they are curious to try something new that they can see others doing. The idea that 'everyone's doing it' may influence some people to leave their better judgment, or their common sense, behind.

"Keeping up with the Joneses" is the adult description of peer pressure. It's the push that adults have from society to own the big house, a nice car and all the trimmings. While these things aren't necessarily bad in and of themselves, what it takes to get them might be. If we start sacrificing relationships for material goods, we'll end up missing out on what really matters in life. We should be more concerned about the people in our lives than keeping up with the Joneses.

Too often we race around acquiring more material possessions, responding to social pressure and simply trying to impress people. Then when people respond to the impression we create, this inflates our self-esteem. But for how long and at what cost? Our closets are bursting at the seams, our credit cards are at or over their limit and for some of us, retail therapy is still our chosen form of medication!

The only difference between adulthood and childhood peer pressure is that adults have a little more money and a little more power. When we go shopping, we are influenced in what we buy because we understand we may be judged on the things that we have and the clothes we wear.

However, teenagers are identified as those most 'at risk' of negative peer pressure, not because they are necessarily subject to more social pressures than other age groups, but that the type of peer pressure they have to deal with is often extremely difficult to ignore.

Since our teenage years are a testing ground for adulthood, it is very common for the peer pressures faced by teenagers to engender behavior that is anti-social, rebellious or boundary pushing. It's all part of growing up and learning how to make the right choices for ourselves.

Negative peer pressure that isn't dealt with during the teenage years usually surfaces again throughout adulthood. What once was, "If you don't do this for me, then I won't be your friend anymore" will inevitably become, "If you don't drive a nice car, have an influential job and wear designer clothes, then I won't socialize with you anymore."

The realization of peer pressure hits home when you are in the company of people you respect, but perhaps disagree with. The power of peer pressure may cause you to say something you don't really mean in order to win their approval and affirmation. Often we cave into this kind of pressure — to our detriment. There are times, of course, when you choose to agree with someone in order to bring peace to a situation, when that particular issue doesn't really matter. But what happens when there are times that you are called on to compromise your principles? What do you do?

Peer pressure tries to dictate to us who we should be and what we should do. People who are easily led and not self-confident depend excessively on the approval of others in order to feel good about themselves. Everyone is susceptible to peer pressure and it takes courage to stand, or as the case may be, remain seated, for your convictions.

Pressure brings out what is really inside us. We will all feel pressure, but what we produce is ultimately our own responsibility, security or insecurity.

Pinocchio

In this version of *Pinocchio* we can see the influence of affluence.

Pinocchio wanted to follow others to have what they had, at any cost. He didn't have the confidence and self-esteem to reject negative social pressure. He was influenced by affluence and his so-called friend led him astray.

Apart from peer pressure, *Pinocchio* also represents the runaway that is sometimes present in all of us who want to depart from any sense of responsibility for the mess we may find ourselves in — whether self-inflicted or otherwise.

Pinocchio was a runaway who wanted to escape to a world that he hoped would make him feel better about himself. Escapism is an outcome of poor self-esteem, and it's not just teenagers who run away. The spirit of the runaway is alive and thriving in many adult lives.

People can be present in body yet absent in mind, will and emotion because of poor self-esteem. Running away, or living in denial, is as much a state of mind as it is a physical action.

Affluenza

So, who are the Joneses anyway, and why are we trying to keep up with them? Apparently they started out in 1879 as a snobby family standing apart from the crowd in England. In *Memoirs of a Station Master*, E.J. Simmons commented on the way people interacted at a public meeting place — the railway station. He wrote, '*The Joneses, who don't associate with the Robinsons, meet there.*'

His observation related to class distinction. One way of dealing with that particular gulf of class difference has been to keep up with the Joneses by buying material possessions that make people look as though they are part of a world that they are not. This is a type of peer pressure called '*affluenza,*' defined by psychotherapist Jessie H. O'Neill as, 'The bloated, sluggish and unfulfilled feeling that results from efforts to keep up with the Joneses.'

It is also an epidemic whose symptoms are stress, overwork, waste and indebtedness caused by a relentless pursuit of the American dream of accumulating 'things.' It is a misguided notion that we can buy our way into who we want to be and it usually ends up with us bankrupt: physically and emotionally. Why allow yourself to be reduced to the '*haves*' and '*have nots*' in life?

Among the symptoms of *affluenza* which O'Neill has identified are:

★   a loss of personal and professional productivity
★   an inability to delay gratification or tolerate frustration
★   a false sense of entitlement
★   low self-esteem and low self-worth
★   loss of self-confidence
★   preoccupation with externals
★   depression
★   self-absorption.

The difference between affluence and influence is huge. Affluence is simply the accumulation of wealth and material objects. Influence is the potential reach of your life and its effect on others.

The relentless pursuit of money has a corrupting influence, if not in a criminal sense, at least in a moral sense of taking our eyes off the things that really matter, like relationships and our own personal wellbeing. What's important is not what we do or don't have, but rather our perspective on material possessions in our life.

Take a good hard look in the mirror and ask why you do what you do, and then assess the impact that the desire for possessions is having on your life. Healthy self-esteem does not come from us acquiring more and more material possessions. Even the poor, who may appear to have no power, no material wealth, no acclaim and no influence, can internally possess all the riches of heaven itself and a tremendously healthy self-esteem.

All the trappings of wealth and power that we either have and bask in, or wish we had and strive for, are empty in themselves. There is no lasting value to them. If we are caught up in them we lose a sense of personal value. Even as we go about our business, they are fading away. You really can't take any of it with you, and sometimes you can't even keep it while you're here. It's true that we all need material things for day-to-day living, but it is so easy to get caught up in the race of continually getting more and so be snared in a trap of discontentment.

When oil tycoon John D. Rockefeller was once asked how much money he thought was enough, he answered, "Just a little bit more." This demonstrates that it doesn't matter where you are on the scale of wealth, it's so easy to think, "If only my circumstances in life could be different." When we don't appreciate the life we have, we focus on what we don't have rather than what we do have. We want to have all the stuff everyone else has, and we usually pay dearly for this desire.

If we want to create wealth in our lives in order to be able to help other people, then I believe that is a legitimate reason to work hard and earn much! To feather our own nest and to neglect the nest of our neighbor is incredibly selfish and damaging to us. We were born to help others and it's when we learn to share what we have that we tend to become less consumed with materialism and more consumed with helping and contributing to others.

To counter the consumer message, we need to focus on genuine contentment. This comes from love and acceptance and is arguably both the strongest human need and the strongest motivator. Unconditional love is a priceless gift no money can buy.

Our need for acceptance and affirmation by our friends and peers can drive us to do things that we know may hurt us and others. This is an issue we all must face as potential pain doesn't seem to stop many of us!

Following are some suggestions to help relieve the pressure of materialism and acceptance, if that is what is weighing you down:

1. Before you buy, ask yourself: do I really need it?
2. Consider: how many hours will I have to work to pay for it?
3. Avoid unnecessary visits to shopping centers.
4. Splurge consciously, not accidentally.
5. Create a budget and resolve to get out of debt.

Escapism

Sometimes the need for approval also leads us to want to fabricate parts of our life in order to be accepted. We can tend to live like puppets of other people's opinions if we don't form our own. Negative peer pressure causes people to become like puppets, doing and saying what they think will make them acceptable, whether good or bad, the truth or lies.

People who are prone to succumb to peer pressure usually don't realize a good thing when they have it. They tend to go through life thinking that they don't need character development — just more stuff and more acceptance. This attitude focuses on everything but the real issue. These people become sucked in by so-called friends who promise the earth but only deliver pain.

Pinocchio's story reminds me of another story about a reckless, prodigal son. He was a young man who ran away from a good home where he was loved and decided to follow the course of "If it feels good, do it" — which caused him to pay a high cost for low living. He eventually saw his mistake and returned home, where he was greeted with grace and forgiveness from his father.

Peer pressure can cause people to do ridiculous, careless and thoughtless things. Running away from home to escape from their problems falls into this category. A person's self-esteem and body image doesn't change by running away. They will only change and grow in a secure environment.

Facing your problems means coming clean with yourself and everyone around you. The truth will set you free. Telling lies always leads to more lies, and there is no way out of the cycle unless you stop. Remember the saying, "Oh what a tangled web we weave when first we practice to deceive!" When we habitually lie, we become more trapped. A lifestyle of fabrication will do nothing to build your self-esteem; rather, it is guaranteed to destroy it.

It's time to consider replacing some bad habits:

1. Replace consumerism with contentment.
2. Replace running away with facing your problems.
3. Replace lying with the truth.

Peer pressure can cause us to feel as though we need to be someone else and this negative road inevitably leads to a life of denial and lies. When you decide to be honest and to do what is right by your own conscience and right by your fellow 'man', you will find a positive momentum in your life which will fast-track you upwards. If, however, you decide to be dishonest and to continually transgress your conscience, you will find a negative momentum in your life which will fast-track you downwards. And you cannot fight this kind of gravity! Remember, if you stand your ground and do what you know is right, you'll never regret it.

It can be hard to walk away from negative peer pressure, but it can be done. Paying attention to your own feelings and beliefs about what is right and wrong can help you determine the right thing to do. Having strong convictions in life helps you stand firm, walk away and resist doing something when you know better.

Insecurity

As social pressure influences you to do that which you don't want to do, insecurity influences you not to do that which you want to do. And insecurity is usually at the root of succumbing to peer pressure. Not being sure of who you are will cause you to want to gain security from what other people say about you.

Insecurity is something that we all face at some time in our lives. Broadly speaking, security is the state of being free from a sense of fear and doubt about who we are.

When we are seeking security, we are seeking a sense of our own value. We believe that our value depends on the work we do, on our financial status, on our appearance, or on our relationships, but our value is more deeply based than any of this.

Insecure people live with dreadful anxiety and paranoia about what everyone is thinking about them. What a way to live! Being yourself is much easier, more releasing and freeing. Insecurity and the need for constant affirmation from others is a trap that will keep us living in an unreal world.

We can all be guilty of distorting reality to try to create our own version of reality — one we think will meet our needs — and we sometimes look for people who will tell us what we want to hear.

Many people want to be cool and have the hottest body and the latest stuff to maintain their security. For example, many people have status symbol toys, the latest everything, but do they really need them? There's nothing wrong with owning 'things,' it's just not healthy to desire to own things in order to establish your identity.

Insecurity is about gaining acceptability. You may feel like you've got to be a style leader, but at what cost, and how will you keep it up? There is a deep longing in each of us to belong and that's normal and understandable, but some people confuse this longing for wanting to be known or famous and they will go to any lengths to see that realized. An unhealthy desire to be instantly known and accepted robs people of their security, identity, self-esteem and self-worth.

insecurity
Check List

1. You think someone's not going to like you for no logical reason.

2. You act like someone you're not.

3. You wish you looked different.

4. Insecurity shows in your facial expressions.

5. You live an inward, introspective life, always thinking about yourself and your problems.

security
Check List

1.   You know who you are and where you're going.

2.   You are not afraid to speak up for your convictions.

3.   You are often a quiet achiever.

4.   You understand that your value is based on who you are and not what people say you are.

5.   You live an outward-focused life, caring for the needs of others as well as yourself.

In order to gain freedom from insecurity, you must focus on some important foundational keys:

1. Find your value internally, not externally.
2. Don't over-spend on 'here today and gone tomorrow' things.
3. Don't listen to people who just tell you what you want to hear.
4. Find friends who will be honest with you.
5. Be honest with your friends.
6. Don't pretend to be someone you are not.
7. Walk confidently in who you really are.
8. Build balance into your life by improving your body and soul.
9. Don't be afraid to be transparent.
10. Trust the truth, as it will always set you free.

Confidence

Confidence is attractive and it is essential to healthy self-esteem. We were all born with confidence, but sometimes life's happenings can knock it out of us. Confidence is often misunderstood.

Let's take a look at what confidence is and what confidence is not, and how you can build it into your life, so that the real you can be expressed with a natural confidence and ease.

confidence
Is

1.   Being sure of who you are

2.   Boldness

3.   Assurance

4.   Intimacy

5.   Openness

6.   Security

7.   Positive and accurate self-talk

8.   Friendliness

9.   Graciousness

10. Purposefulness

confidence
Is Not

1. Trying to be someone else

2. Arrogance

3. Cockiness

4. Self-absorption

5. Self-promotion

6. Insecurity

7. Negative and inaccurate self-talk

8. Attention seeking

9. Boasting

10. Hiding one's true self.

confidence
Builders

1. Acknowledge that you are highly valuable.

2. Don't let other people's opinions rule your life.

3. Forgive all the people who have hurt you, and forgive   yourself.

4. Always choose with your future in mind. Don't make hasty decisions — think first.

5. Look in the mirror and don't cringe. Accept who you are and improve what you can without becoming obsessive.

6. Never settle for Mr. Okay or Ms. Average.

7. Always listen to wise people who know better than you.

8. Don't isolate yourself from good friends when life gets tough.

9. Learn to say no when you are tempted to compromise.

10. Don't throw away your confidence because it carries with it a great reward.

Leadership

I can't say that I am the 'easily led' type, but during my lifetime I have definitely done my fair share of leading others who were easily led. At school, most of it was positive, but some of it I am fairly ashamed of today. I was the ringleader and used to get not only myself but a number of my friends into mischief. Being a leader is a real responsibility. If you are a genuine leader, people will be following you.

Once you understand that all of us have people who are looking to us for cues in life, it's important to make sure that where we lead people will cause them to grow rather than fall into the traps and pitfalls of life. We should aim to become cultivators of positive peer pressure.

When we don't have all that we think we should have, we naturally want more. We may not want to be super-rich, but we do want to be more comfortable. We become absorbed with getting what we don't have and this is when we need to turn our attention to being grateful for what we do have. There is great power in thankfulness. Take a look at what you do have and be grateful.

I have learned that contentment is a priceless condition and sometimes a hard place to reach and maintain. Envy, that green-eyed monster, can subtly creep into our hearts if we allow it and it will destroy our self-esteem. (There's more on that subject in Chapter 10.) I value the leadership that is part of my life and I choose to use that gift of leadership to help others develop a healthy self-esteem and identity.

Transparency

Being honest with yourself is essential if you want to live the happily ever after life. Being transparent is neither shameful nor weak. It is in fact a great strength. You need to have a healthy appreciation for who you really are in order to develop healthy, positive relationships. And you can only do this from a position of security.

Go ahead and be you and don't be afraid of the truth. Don't be afraid of constructive observation and criticism and let your image be based on the real you, not on what you think people want to see. Trying to maintain an image, at any age, can be a real trap.

There's nothing wrong with having a positive image, but trying or striving to maintain an image that is not true to who you are will inevitably show. Reputation or credibility is something that has to be built over time and it's based on not just what you do and what you look like, but on who you are.

Mariah Carey is a very beautiful and successful singer–songwriter, but her life has not been without its challenges. Even with all the success in the world, it doesn't matter when you can't see who you really are. It has been widely reported that she has battled and continues to battle the same insecurities as everyone else. A magazine article I read about Mariah discussed her being one of the most successful female singers of all time. Mariah has sold millions of albums and had fifteen number one hits (bettered only by Elvis and The Beatles). She's incredibly wealthy and is the only artist to have had a number one hit each year in the 1990s— thus was named the Artist of the Decade.

With all the money and fame in the world, even with her great achievements, it still hasn't brought her a sense of belonging or identity. Mariah's parents separated when she was very young and she grew up with little to survive on. Her childhood is more real to her than her fame and fortune. Although she knows she is very blessed, she still feels like the same insecure kid who lived in the worst house in the street, who didn't wear the right clothes or have any of the things other kids did.

Mariah's story goes to show that no matter how much you surround yourself or try to prop yourself up with 'stuff,' you still need to decide to like and respect yourself, to truly be content and secure. When we like ourselves and when we are very comfortable with being ourselves, we won't be easily changed or led astray.

When we look at the people who are most respected by their peers, we will usually find people who are confident and who will stand up for themselves and others and they generally appear to have strong personal values. And when you value yourself, you are able to value others in return. In order for our self-esteem to develop well and flourish, we have a responsibility to lead wisely and to follow only those who are going to be a positive influence in our lives.

Remember the Truth:
confidence enables you to decide for yourself.

the paradox of our time in history

The paradox of our time in history is that ...
We have taller buildings but shorter tempers,
Wider freeways, but narrower viewpoints.
We spend more, but have less. We buy more, but enjoy less.
We have bigger houses and smaller families,
More conveniences, but less time.
We have more degrees but less sense, more knowledge,
But less judgment, more experts, yet more problems,
More medicine, but less wellness.
We drink too much, smoke too much, spend too recklessly,
Laugh too little, drive too fast, get too angry,
Stay up too late, get up too tired, read too little,
Watch TV too much, and pray too seldom.
We have multiplied our possessions, but reduced our values.
We talk too much, love too seldom, and hate too often.
We've learned how to make a living, but not a life.
We've added years to life, not life to years.
We've been all the way to the moon and back,
But have trouble crossing the street to meet a new neighbor.
We conquered outer space but not inner space
We've done larger things, but not better things.
We've cleaned up the air, but polluted the soul.
We've conquered the atom, but not our prejudice.
We write more, but learn less. We plan more, but accomplish less.
We've learned to rush, but not to wait ...
These are the days of two incomes but more divorce
Fancier houses, but broken homes.
These are days of quick trips, disposable diapers,
Throwaway morality, one-night stands,
Overweight bodies and pills that do everything from cheer, to quiet, to kill.
It is a time where there is much in the showroom window
And nothing in the stockroom. Indeed, truly, these are the times.
BOB MOOREHEAD

10 keys to freedom

[from people pleasing]

Expect that applying some of these keys will shake up your relationships. Some may even crumble, but the true and worthwhile relationships will stand the test. It will take concentration and commitment to find the keyhole to unlock the truth — remember, FREEDOM is the goal.

1. Choose your friends wisely. Don't spend time with fools unless you are going to influence them positively. Remember that you can't buy love, friendship, genuine acceptance or happiness; if you relax and be YOU, you will find these things finding you.

2. Become a leader and start to set positive trends for others to follow. You are the leader of YOU.

3. Set and keep to a budget.

4. Don't lie or it will catch up with you eventually — what goes around comes around.

5. Always remain true to yourself and to your conscience.

6. Replace running away with facing the truth.

7. Set standards and values for your own life. Know who you want to be and you will be less likely to become someone you don't want to be.

8. Stand up and speak up for what you believe in — do it feeling afraid if you have to.

9. Learn to say no, even when you are tempted to compromise.

10. Replace consumerism with contentment.

body & soul
[action plan]

Body

Make some decisions for yourself about how you spend your money and what you really need, regardless of pressure you may feel from others. Confidently and securely stand your ground and don't shrink or run away.

Soul

Assess regularly whether you are truly living for what you believe in, rather than what everyone else wants for your life. Be committed to your soul flourishing. Develop the ability to discern the influences in your life and to establish what is healthy and unhealthy, and then believe for the strength to draw any necessary lines.

**My goal is Freedom
FROM PEOPLE PLEASING**

my notes

[write your thoughts]

chapter five

The Cyber Social Club

freedom from social media pressure
[be yourself online and offline]

aladdin

Once upon a time there was a handsome and good-hearted boy named Aladdin. When he was still very young, tragedy struck his family leaving him orphaned and living on the streets near the market place. Though life was hard and Aladdin didn't always have enough to eat, he always shared what we had with other young orphans. Years passed and one day Aladdin saw a beautiful girl wandering through the market. He thought he must talk to her, but as he approached her he realized that she was the Princess, Jasmine. She was very beautiful, smart and kind. She had lovely clothes and all the finest things, but because Aladdin was poor and his clothes were old and worn, he felt that he wasn't good enough to talk to her. As he walked away frustrated, he realized he was very hungry. Although he knew stealing was wrong, he decided to take a loaf of bread.

Aladdin was caught breaking the law and as punishment for his crime was forced as a slave to go on an expedition to nearby ruins with a very devious man. Once they arrived, Aladdin was forced to enter the very dangerous ruins to find the treasure the devious man so greatly desired. Aladdin used his quick footing to make it through dangerous mazes until deep in the ruins he found the treasure. It was an old oil lamp! And though it didn't look like much to Aladdin, he reached for it to take it back to his master. As he did, Aladdin triggered a trap and all the ruins began tumbling down around him, blocking all the exits. He was now stuck underground! He picked up the oil lamp and wiped the dust off. The lamp started to rattle and shake, and before his very eyes a magnificent genie appeared from out of the lamp! The genie whirled about in the cavern. "I am your Genie!" he said in a powerful and friendly voice. The genie lifted Aladdin up and they flew away. They soared far into the sky and landed safely. "What is it that you wish for? I can grant you three wishes." Aladdin stood stunned, could he really have whatever he wanted? Aladdin remembered the beautiful princess and wanted to make her love him. The genie said, " I have the power to grant you anything you want, but I cannot make anyone love you. Love comes from a person's free will." Aladdin thought to himself that if he *appeared* to have a better life, one filled with adventure and wealth, that the princess would most certainly love him. So Aladdin used his first two wishes to make him appear to be a prince. But not just any prince, Aladdin wished to be the most fun, wealthy, well dressed, adventurous prince he could imagine. The genie sighed as he granted these wishes, knowing that all the appearance of fame and wealth would never bring real love into Aladdin's life.

Aladdin paraded through the old market place with his new appearance, but Princess Jasmine paid no attention to him at all. Aladdin tried harder, and bombarded her with his flashy lifestyle. But the princess had no interest in this at all.

Saddened, Aladdin found comfort in talking with the genie. The genie kindly explained to Aladdin that while he had wanted to appear to be so great, he had failed to see how amazing he really was. As the genie spoke kindness and truth to Aladdin, he began to remember who he truly was. Aladdin lifted his head and his eyes began to shine, he turned to the genie and said, "Genie, I wish for freedom. The freedom to live my life to help people, not to impress them." The genie was overjoyed as he granted this last wish.

Aladdin went back to the market place and used his freedom to help the other poor orphans by showing them the value of their lives. Instead of trying to make himself appear important, he did important things that made a difference. Princess Jasmine heard of the amazing things Aladdin was doing to help the orphans and she could not wait to be a part of it. And together they lived helping others happily ever after.

the end

Fact

The highlight reels of our friends and favorite celebrities are ever before us.

truth

What we see isn't necessarily what is real.

mirror mirror on the wall ...

why do I feel so much pressure from social media?

Once upon a time, there was no Facebook, Twitter, Instagram or YouTube. Our lives did not revolve around a constant stream of status updates, tweets, videos and filtered photos. That was just 10 years ago. This constant stream of words and images that we now live with can provide us with countless hours of entertainment and a form of 'connection' with the outside world. Yet sometimes that steady feed of status updates can overwhelm us. Sometimes what we see and read from all the people we follow on social media via the apps and websites we access on our smart phones, tablets and computer screens can make us feel like we don't measure up.

Just like the character Aladdin in my re-imagined version of the classic fairy tale, we may start to become dissatisfied with our real, off-screen lives. Compared to everyone else's feed, we may start to view our lives as boring and going nowhere. As our perspective is distorted by this often subconscious act of comparison, we may start to believe that we need to throw a more appealing filter over our real lives, in order to get more 'likes' or 'follows', or simply to feel more 'normal'.

The Evolution of Social Media

1. **Myspace : launched August 2003**
    Myspace is a social networking service with a strong music emphasis. Myspace was founded in 2003 by Chris DeWolfe and Tom Anderson, and was later acquired by News Corporation in July 2005 for $580 million. Myspace was once the most visited social networking site in the world. Since 2008, the number of Myspace users has declined steadily in spite of several redesigns.

2. **Facebook : launched February 2004**
    Facebook is an online social networking service, founded by Mark Zuckerberg with his college roommates and fellow Harvard University students Eduardo Saverin, Andrew McCollum, Dustin Moskovitz and Chris Hughes. Facebook had over 1.3 billion active

users as of June 2014. Due to the large volume of data collected about users, the service's privacy policies have faced scrutiny, among other criticisms. Facebook, Inc. held its initial public offering in February 2012 and began selling stock to the public three months later, reaching a peak market capitalization of $104 billion.

3. **Twitter : launched July 2006**
   Twitter is an online social networking service that enables users to send and read short 140-character messages called "tweets". Twitter was created by Jack Dorsey, Evan Williams, Biz Stone and Noah Glass. As of July 2014, Twitter has more than 500 million users, out of which more than 271 million are active users.

4. **Tumblr : launched February 2007**
   Tumblr is a microblogging platform and social networking website founded by David Karp and owned by Yahoo! Inc. The service allows users to post multimedia and other content to a short-form blog. Within two weeks of Tumblr's launch, the service had gained 75,000 users. In 2013 Yahoo! acquired Tumblr, for approximately $1.1 billion. As of November 1, 2014, Tumblr hosts over 209.3 million blogs.

5. **Pinterest : launched March 2010**
   Pinterest is a web and mobile application company that offers a visual discovery, collection, sharing, and storage tool. Users create and share the collections of visual bookmarks (boards). The site was founded by Ben Silbermann, Paul Sciarra and Evan Sharp. The website has proven especially popular among women. In May 2014, Pinterest was valued at $5 billion.

6. **Instagram : launched October 2010**
   Instagram is an online mobile photo-sharing, video-sharing and social networking service that enables its users to take pictures and videos, and share them on a variety of social networking platforms. Instagram was created by Kevin Systrom and Mike Krieger. The service was acquired by Facebook in April 2012 for approximately US$1 billion in cash and stock. As of September

2013, the company announced a total of more than 150 million monthly active users. 90% of Instagram's 150 million users are under the age of 35.

7. Snapchat : launched September 2011

Snapchat is a photo messaging application developed by Evan Spiegel, Bobby Murphy, and Reggie Brown, then Stanford University students. Using the application, users can take photos, record videos, add text and drawings, and send them to a controlled list of recipients. These sent photographs and videos are known as "Snaps". Users set a time limit for how long recipients can view their Snaps (as of April 2014, the range is from 1 to 10 seconds), after which they will be hidden from the recipient's device and deleted from Snapchat's servers. According to Snapchat in May 2014, the app's users were sending 700 million photos and videos per day, while Snapchat Stories content was being viewed 500 million times per day. In late August 2014, the company was valued at US$10 billion. On May 9, 2013, Snapchat's blog responded to the speculation regarding the retrieval of its app's images: *"If you've ever tried to recover lost data after accidentally deleting a drive or maybe watched an episode of CSI, you might know that with the right forensic tools, it's sometimes possible to retrieve data after it has been deleted. So... you know... keep that in mind before putting any state secrets in your selfies :)"*

THE SELFIE

A **selfie** is a self-portrait photograph, typically taken with a hand-held digital camera or camera phone. Selfies are often shared on social networking services such as Facebook, Instagram, Twitter or Snapchat. Most selfies are taken with a camera held at arm's length or pointed at a mirror, rather than by using a self-timer. Selfies are appealing because they are easy to create and share and they give self-photographers control over how they present themselves.

The popularity of selfies in social media has been astounding. By the end of 2012, *Time* magazine considered the word "selfie" one of the "top 10 buzzwords" of that year. Instagram has over 53 million photos tagged with the hashtag #selfie. The word "selfie" was mentioned in Facebook status updates over 368,000 times during a one week period in October 2013. During the same period on Twitter, the hashtag #selfie was used in more than 150,000 tweets.

SELFIE-ESTEEM

Today.com contributor, Melissa Dahl writes about "Selfie-esteem." In the "Ideal to Real TODAY/AOL Body Image Survey", teenage girls revealed something unexpected: 65 percent said seeing their selfies on social media actually boosts their confidence. And 40 percent of all teens say social media helps "me present my best face to the world."

These findings echo escalating social science on the real impact of social media on self-image. Selfies are incredibly important to teenagers, because they provide a way to control the image of themselves that they're showing to the world.

"It's the first time you get to be the photographer *and* the subject of the photograph," says Pamela Rutledge, director of the Media Psychology Research Center, who has written extensively about this particular subject, especially as it applies to teens and Millennials. "Even though that seems very simple, that's an extraordinary shift, historically. And control makes people believe in themselves."

Psychologists call it self-efficacy—the idea that you can control your own world, "which is a really big deal for the human brain," Rutledge says.

It seems that as long as people are in control of the image, they are somehow more confident. However, in the "TODAY/AOL Body Image Survey", young people acknowledge social media's power to make them feel bad about themselves, especially when they are confronted with beautiful, mostly happy, pictures of other people's lives.

★ 55 percent of girls and 34 percent of teen boys say "overall, social media makes me feel more self-conscious about my appearance."

★ 58 percent of teen girls say "seeing pictures of other people living glamorous-looking lives on social media makes me feel bad about myself." Only 19 percent of teen boys have the same reaction.

★ 30 percent of all teens say social media means they always need to be "camera-ready."

Teens and Social Media

Adolescence is an important period of rapid development and the constant flood of texts and social media have become primary relational tools. Young people who are addicted to technology usually show signs of anxiety and low self-esteem, over those who aren't.

Teens are experts in keeping occupied. We rarely hear words citing boredom, as the internet provides pathways of activity and escape for all who stay online; texting, sharing, scrolling. Modern teens are learning to communicate while looking at a screen rather than another person.

"As a species we are very highly attuned to reading social cues," says Dr. Catherine Steiner-Adair, a clinical psychologist and author of *The Big Disconnect*. "There's no question kids are missing out on very critical social skills. In a way, texting and online communicating—it's not like it creates a nonverbal learning disability, but it puts everybody in a nonverbal disabled context, where body language, facial expression, and even the smallest kinds of vocal reactions are rendered invisible."

Whether making a new friend or maintaining existing relationships, true friendships require time, energy and a certain amount of risk-taking. Relationship building and problem solving is always best done in person.

"Part of healthy self-esteem is knowing how to say what you think and feel even when you're in disagreement with other people or it feels emotionally risky," notes Dr. Steiner-Adair.

When we only relate to people via texts, emails and direct messaging, we lose the essence of human contact, which provides authenticity and vulnerability. Texting is too easy as it can be a one-way dialogue without the need for a timely response. Because techno-relationships don't have to be built in real time, we can string people along into wondering whether we are choosing to ignore them or not.

It is no wonder kids think calling someone and having a telephone conversation is way too intense, especially when they are used to the guarded, and very controlled world of techno-communication.

Cyberbullying and the Imposter Syndrome

One big indirect danger that comes with communication is that it is now easier than ever to be cruel at a whole new level. "Kids text all sorts of things that you would never in a million years contemplate saying to anyone's face," says Dr. Donna Wick, a clinical and developmental psychologist who runs "Mind to Mind Parent." She notes that this seems to be especially true of girls, who typically don't like to disagree with each other in "real life."

Dr. Steiner-Adair agrees that girls are particularly at risk. "Girls are socialized more to compare themselves to other people, girls in particular, to develop their identities, so it makes them more vulnerable to the downside of all this." She warns that a lack of solid self-esteem is often to blame. "We forget that relational aggression comes from insecurity and feeling awful about yourself, and wanting to put other people down so you feel better."

Being accepted and liked by peers is important to young people, and having Facebook or Instagram "likes" provides a means of polling data that causes girls to want to look better than each other and boys to out-do each other. The choice of a single photo to post can be an agonizing experience.

"Adolescence and the early twenties in particular are the years in which you are acutely aware of the contrasts between who you appear to be and who you think you are," says Dr. Wick. "It's similar to the 'imposter syndrome' in psychology. As you get older and acquire more mastery, you begin to realize that you actually are good at some things, and then you feel that gap hopefully narrow. But imagine having your deepest darkest fear be that you aren't as good as you look, and then imagine needing to look that good all the time! It's exhausting."

As Dr. Steiner-Adair explains, "Self-esteem comes from consolidating who you are." The more identities you have, and the more time you spend pretending to be someone you aren't, the harder it's going to be to feel good about yourself.

Stalking (and being ignored)

A new phenomenon that has arrived with the technological era is that we are never really alone and we can provide all details of our life 24/7, with the click of an update. What we're watching, listening to, eating and where we are at any given time, can be out there for the world to see.

Kids are never out of reach of text messaging which results in hyper-connectivity with each other. What used to be long telephone conversations late at night, with a phone and a cord attached, has now become mobile, instant and constant.

Dr. Wick says that kids never get a break from their relationships, which can produce anxiety. "Everyone needs a respite from the demands of intimacy and connection; time alone to regroup, replenish and just chill out. When you don't have that, it's easy to become emotionally depleted, fertile ground for anxiety to breed."

Being highly connected leaves room for hurt. Kids know, with depressing certainty, when they are being ignored by friends. The silent treatment might be intentional or it could be a more typical result of online relationships that are fast and furious; starting out strong but soon fading away.

"In the old days when a boy was going to break up with you, he had to have a conversation with you. Or at least he had to call," says Dr. Wick. "These days he might just disappear from your screen, and you never get to have the 'What did I do?' conversation." Kids are often left imagining the worst about themselves.

What should parents do?

The best thing parents should do is to be a healthy example to their kids, spending adequate time away from smartphones. Most of us check our phones and email too much, out of either real interest or nervous habit. Our kids need to see our faces and to learn healthy communication and relationship building from us. Kids need to know we are available to talk about their day and help them with their problems.

While the internet can provide more information than any human on planet earth, it cannot provide values. We need human contact to help us process all the information that flows towards us on a daily basis.

Building healthy self-esteem and resilience requires building a life that includes physical and emotional involvement, such as sport, music, team interaction – anything that is of interest that can build healthy confidence. We need to be confident in who we are and what we do, not just in how we look and whether others will approve of us or not.

Look Up
by Gary Turk

I have 422 friends yet I am lonely
I speak to all of them every day yet none of them really know me
The problem I have sits in the space in-between
Looking into their eyes or at a name on a screen
I took a step back and opened my eyes
I looked round and realized
This media we call social is anything but
when we open our computers and it's our doors we shut
All this technology we have it's just an illusion
Community, companionship, a sense of inclusion
When you step away from this device of delusion
You awaken to see a world of confusion
A world where we're slaves to the technology we mastered
Where information gets sold by some rich, greedy 'man'
A world of self-interest, self-image, self-promotion
Where we all share our best bits but leave out the emotion
We're at our most happy with an experience we share
But is it the same if no one is there?
Be there for your friends and they'll be there too
But no one will be if a group message will do
We edit and exaggerate, crave adulation
We pretend not to notice the social isolation
We put our words into order till our lives are glistening
We don't even know if anyone is listening
Being alone isn't the problem let me just emphasize
If you read a book, paint a picture, or do some exercise
You're being productive and present not reserved and reclused
You're being awake and attentive and putting your time to good use
So when you're in public and you start to feel alone
Put your hands behind your head, step away from the phone
You don't need to stare at your menu or at your contact list
Just talk to one another, learn to co-exist
I can't stand to hear the silence of a busy commuter train
When no one wants to talk for the fear of looking insane
We're becoming unsocial, it no longer satisfies
To engage with one another and look into someone's eyes.

We're surrounded by children who since they were born
Have watched us living like robots and think it's the norm
It's not very likely you'll make world's greatest Dad
If you can't entertain a child without using an iPad
When I was a child I'd never be home
I'd wear holes in my trainers and graze up my knees
Or build our own clubhouse high up in the trees
Now the park is so quiet it gives me a chill
See no children outside and the swings hanging still
There's no skipping, no hopscotch, no church and no steeple
We're a generation of idiots, smart phones and dumb people
So look up from your phone, shut down the display
Take in your surroundings, make the most of today
Just one real connection is all it can take
To show you the difference that being there can make
Be there in the moment as she gives you the look
That you remember forever as when love overtook
The time she first held your hand or first kissed your lips
The time you first disagreed but still loved her to bits
The time you don't have to tell hundreds of what you've just done
Because you want to share this moment with just this one.
The time you sell your computer so you can buy a ring
For the girl of your dreams who is now the real thing
The time you want to start a family and the moment when
You first hold your little girl and get to fall in love again
The time she keeps you up at nights and all you want is rest
And the time you wipe away the tears as your baby flees the nest
The time your baby girl returns with a boy for you to hold
And the time he calls you Granddad and makes you feel real old
The time you take in all you've made when you're giving life attention
And how you're real glad you didn't waste it by looking down at some
invention
The time you hold your wife's hand, sit down beside her bed.
You tell her that you love her, lay a kiss upon her head.
She then whispers to you quietly as her heart gives a final beat
That she's lucky she got stopped by that lost boy in the street
But none of these times ever happened. You never had any of this
When you're too busy looking down, you don't see the chances you miss
So look up from your phones, shut down those displays
We have a finite existence, a set number of days

Don't waste your life getting caught in the net
because when the end comes, nothing's worse than regret
I am guilty too of being part of this machine
this digital world we are heard but not seen
where we type as we talk and read as we chat
where we spend hours together without making eye-contact
So don't give in to a life where you follow the hype
Give people your love, don't give them your "like"
Disconnect from the need to be heard and defined
Go out into the world, leave distractions behind
Look up from your phone, shut down the display
Stop watching this video, live life the real way.

"Social Media Cover Story vs Real Story"

by Kerri Weems

Adapted from a presentation given at IMAGINE Conference 2014

Social media is a big part of the world we live in today, and actually has a lot of potential for good. The problem is that it's just 'out there', without any kind of regulation. Once upon a time you would at least try to restrain yourself from saying things that weren't appropriate. Now you have to restrain yourself from 'tweeting' something that's not appropriate. Social media has given us an instant platform to say whatever comes to our minds.

In the online world, whenever you're not looking at someone face to face, it is all too easy to dehumanize a person, and say things to them or about them that you would never ever say to them in person. This is probably one of the most destructive aspects of social media.

However, there are a lot of good things about social media. If it's used with wisdom, it gives people the opportunity to speak to situations directly and can bring awareness to important issues around the world. It can really help in keeping us connected to people we care about, and helps us remember our friends' birthdays. Thank you Facebook!

Cover Stories

On social media, we all have a cover story. It's the best image of ourselves that we want people to believe that we are. It's what psychologists call the 'ideal self'. It is who we want other people to believe that we are, and it's what we project to them.

Social media is essentially our cover story, rather than our real story. If we're not careful, it can cause us to begin to create distance between our inner world, and our outer world.

Real Self vs Ideal Self

Part of the big growth curve of human development is to become what psychologists call 'integrated'. It's very normal to want to achieve, to improve, to become better and to grow. In order to grow, we need to project into what we could be – we need to take time to think about what we could become if we put in some effort. But when we start to have two different parts of who we are [our real self vs our ideal self], and we don't bring those things into alignment, we become fractured people.

The journey of becoming integrated is where our real story, and our cover story move closer together, and become the same thing. We become more authentic versions of ourselves. Someone once said that 'If you think that you're the customer of Facebook, you're wrong. You are not the customer – you are the product.' On social media we are creating these consumable, 'product' versions of ourselves, to sell if you will, to others. And if we don't realize that what we're putting out may not actually be authentically us, we can start to have this double life, without being aware of it.

The word *integrity* comes from the word *'integer'*, meaning 'a whole number without fracture'. A number without fracture is a whole number. A person without fracture is a whole person. We are designed to be one whole person, not many different versions of ourselves.

The more we follow an idealized version of ourselves, the less content we become with the real version of ourselves. The more we project and lean into the cover story, the less content we become with our real story. The purpose of becoming whole is really about accepting and loving the real story. It's not about escaping into daydream land, dreaming of the life you wish you had, it's about saying, 'This is the life I have and this is what is amazing about it. This is the body I have, and this is what's awesome about it. This is the mind I have, and this is what is really beautiful about it. This is the spouse I have and this is what is amazing about them.'

It is not healthy for us to love an idealized version of someone; we are meant to love others as they really are. It's very freeing to look at someone, remove the expectations, remove the idealism, and say *'Oh this is who you really are. And you know what, I love you as you really are.'*

Don't be in love with some future perfect version of yourself. It's okay to love yourself as you are, because if you don't love yourself, you can't love other people. It is really true that you can't give what you don't have.

When it comes to social media, one of the best things we can do is to start out with a good strong sense of our own identity before we allow our view of ourselves to be modified by what others are saying online.

I've found that those who judge themselves harshly, are often the first to judge others harshly. I used to think there might be some kind of 'karma' at work, that if we judged others, then that same judgment would be sure to come back to us someday. Then I realized that it's not 'karma' but rather a simple principle, that the measure that you use to judge others is often the same measure you use to judge your own self. Think about the things that bother you most about people. Often those same things are the very things that bother you most about *yourself*. They are judgments that you've made against your self. When you love and accept yourself, you will in turn be more loving and accepting of others.

Real Story vs Cover Story

We must remember how to think critically about what we read. We have access to so much information that it could cause us to worry or become depressed. Studies show there's a direct link to the amount of time that people spend passively viewing social media like Facebook, Twitter and Instagram, and depression levels. Depression actually goes up proportionately to the time spent passively viewing social media. Most of us are engaged in social media in a primarily passive way and it's that kind of relationship to social media that makes depression spike. Here's why: when we are looking at social media, we are looking at someone's highlight reel. We're looking at all the best parts of their life, their cover story. Who is going to post the real story? Do you want to see photos of me brushing my teeth, or tying my shoes, thinking about stuff, making a sauce on the stove? People are posting what they think is most interesting about their lives - their highlight reel and cover story.

Highlight Reel vs Game Film

Don't fall into the trap of comparing your game film to someone's highlight reel. Our game film is where we see ourselves getting knocked down, missing plays, messing up the kick, missing a tackle, getting knocked around, and everyone else looks like they're out there changing the world. It's so easy to look at what other people are doing and feel like you are missing out, or that you're not personally doing enough. Comparison can make us lose our sense of who we are. It can make us lose the love for our real story.

Remember, there is beauty and hope in your real story, and your future is bright – brighter than you can even begin to imagine right now. Rather than comparing your daily activity to someone else's social media feed, take time to focus on building your life. Expect the best for your life, taking it one day at a time. Be the best you that you can be and don't fall into the trap of comparison. Know who you are apart from social media and be strong in that knowledge.

Remember the Truth:
What we see isn't necessarily what is real.

10 keys to freedom

[from pressure to be someone you're not]

When we stop comparing ourselves to everyone else in unhealthy ways we will enjoy our own lives much more.

1.   Remember that it's ok to take a break from social media – you don't have to be on it every day.

2.   Set goals for your life, and make a plan to achieve them. When you're focused on your own journey, it's harder to be distracted or discouraged by what everyone else is doing.

3.   Celebrate the success of others.

4.   Don't believe everything you see or read.

5.   Accept yourself as you are now and give yourself grace to grow.

6.   Don't allow yourself to dwell on any negative comments people may have made about you online. Forgive those who hurt you.

7.   Be brave enough to unfollow and unfriend people that are no longer a positive influence in your life.

8.   Think of ways you can use your influence to help and inspire others.

9.   Celebrate your wins along the way.

10.   Remember that there can only be one you, so be the best you that you can be without obsessing over how well you measure up to the efforts of others.

body & soul
[action plan]

Body

Commit to living an active, healthy life rather than just observing the lives and actions of others on social media. Learn to step away from the computer and put down your electronic devices to take breaks from them. Get moving and enjoy your life!

Soul

Remember that we don't see the everyday struggles of the people that we follow on social media – we are mostly seeing their best moments. Remind yourself not to compare your reality to what other people post about their lives. Unplug and log out of your social media accounts from time to time.

**My goal is Freedom
FROM SOCIAL MEDIA PRESSURE**

my notes

[write your thoughts]

chapter six

Beware of the Big Bad Wolf

freedom from unhealthy relationships
["Boundaries define us.
They define what is me and what is not me."]

little red riding hood

Once upon a time, there was a young woman who lived in a village near the forest. Whenever she went out, the young woman wore a red riding cloak, so everyone in the village called her Little Red Riding Hood.

One morning, Little Red Riding Hood went to visit her grandmother. "Remember, go straight to Grandma's house," her mother cautioned. "Don't dawdle along the way and please don't talk to strangers! The woods are dangerous."

But when Little Red Riding Hood noticed some lovely flowers in the woods, she forgot her promise to her mother and she wandered off, not noticing that it was getting late. Suddenly, a young man dressed in a wolf suit appeared beside her.

"What are you doing out here, young lady?" the wolf asked in a devilishly charming voice, his smile revealing large white teeth.

"I'm on my way to see my Grandma, who lives through the forest, near the brook," Little Red Riding Hood replied trustingly. Little Red Riding Hood had heard about the wolf and his wicked ways, but somehow when she met him she thought that he wasn't really all that bad. Perhaps, she thought, he was just misunderstood.

Then she realized how late she was and quickly excused herself, rushing down the path to her grandma's house. In the meantime, the wolf took a shortcut and arrived at Grandma's house ahead of Little Red, where he stealthily opened the front door and let himself in. He grabbed poor Grandma, gagged her and locked her in a cupboard!

Hurrying to trap his real prey, the wolf rummaged through Grandma's clothes to find a nightgown that would fit him. A few moments later, Red Riding Hood knocked on the door.

When Little Red Riding Hood entered the little cottage, she could barely recognize her grandma.

"Grandma! What big ears and eyes you have," said Little Red Riding Hood as she edged closer to the bed.

"The better to hear and see you with, my dear," replied the wolf.

"But Grandma! What big teeth you have," said Little Red Riding Hood, her voice quivering.

"The better to eat you with, my dear," roared the not-so innocent wolf and he leapt out of the bed and lunged at Little Red.

Almost too late, Little Red Riding Hood realized that the person in the bed was not her grandma, but the wolf. She ran across the room and through the door, shouting, "Help! Wolf!" as loudly as she could.

A woodsman who was chopping logs nearby heard her cry and ran towards the cottage as fast as he could. He grabbed the wolf and tied him up before rescuing Grandma, who was now knocking on the cupboard door.

"Oh Grandma, I was so scared!" sobbed Little Red Riding Hood. "I'll never trust a wolf again!"

The woodsman took the wolf outside and carried him deep into the forest, where he wouldn't bother people any longer, and Little Red Riding Hood, her Grandma and mother were happy to never see him again.

the end

fact

Falling in love is easy.

truth

Staying in love requires commitment.

mirror mirror on the wall ...

why do I pick the worst ones of all?

Relationships! Who needs them? Well — we all do! Finding and maintaining meaningful relationships is an important factor in building healthy self-esteem into our lives. When our relationships are healthy, it's easy to feel a great sense of achievement and reward.

What is not easy, of course, is building healthy relationships. It takes commitment and work to produce healthy relationships and the first place we must start is with ourselves. We've often heard it said, or we may have even said it, "What's a nice girl like her doing with a guy like him?"

A nice girl is with a guy like him perhaps because the nice girl doesn't have a sense of her own worth and value. She's living well below the level that she could be living at and it is more to do with her than the guy. The relationship exists as a result of her poor choice. This is why many nice girls choose guys like him, over and over again. A significant number of people do in fact seem to be attracted to the wrong kind of person for them.

You may feel as though you have a magnet on your forehead that attracts unhealthy relationships. Realizing that fact is a great place to start. When you take personal responsibility and shift the blame from the guy to yourself, you are then empowered to break the cycle of unhealthy relationships and begin to assess how valuable you are and who should and can enter your private world.

When it comes to entering any relationship, no matter what happens, it is important to acknowledge that you have something to do with the relationship. It's called "personal responsibility".

Unhealthy Relationships

It is easy to get emotional and angry when we discover that our partner has different values, beliefs or expectations. What's important to understand is there will always be differences in opinions, and how we handle these differences will determine the health of our relationships and how we feel about ourselves. Some of the issues that have a negative impact on relationships are:

★ Lack of time spent together
★ Lack of communication
★ Lack of understanding of views
★ Different goals or expectations
★ Financial insecurity
★ Bringing up children
★ Inability to resolve conflict
★ Sexual difficulties
★ Different cultural backgrounds
★ Lack of trust
★ Alcohol or drug abuse
★ Affairs
★ Gambling
★ Violence

Everyone who is in a relationship or cares about their relationships may need assistance at some time to help deal with problems and to learn how to improve them. We also need assistance when a relationship breaks down.

There is conflict in all relationships at times and that is important to understand. Being able to deal with conflict and handle differences in opinion is crucial in building healthy relationships. We cannot eliminate conflict completely, but we can manage it constructively.

Little Red Riding Hood

In my version of Little Red Riding Hood, we see that the Big Bad Wolf was ready and waiting to take advantage of Little Red. But just as Little Red had something to do with the predicament she found herself in, we too have to take personal responsibility for our own relationships. For some, the Big Bad Wolf is you! For others, it is a person waiting to jump onto your vulnerability.

Whatever mess you find yourself in as a result of naivety or poor choices, wisdom and wise choices can see you through. When we look at Little Red Riding Hood, we see that innocent Little Red thought she could trust the Big Bad Wolf. She felt sorry for him; after all, he had a bad reputation and she didn't think it was fair. She thought perhaps she could help him become a better person. In my version of the story of Little Red Riding Hood, the young woman forgot the promises she made to her mother about going straight to her grandma's house, because in her naivety she did not understand that the boundaries her mother tried to set would help protect her from contact with the wolf.

Co-dependency

People who tend to be naive about relationships also tend to reflect aspects of co-dependency in their relationships. People who are co-dependent naturally care deeply for people and devote their lives to saving others who are in trouble. They usually try so hard to help and manage someone else's life to save them, but when they fail, their own life tends to fall into a crumpled heap of hopelessness because they lose control.

co—dependent
CHECK LIST

How do you know if you might have a co-dependent type personality?
Read through the following checklist to see how you rate. Try to be
completely honest!

1.   Do you focus solely on wanting others to be happy?

2.   Do you feel responsible for your partner's life?

3.   Do you criticize yourself?

4.   Do you feel excessively guilty and full of shame?

5.   Are you an angry and nagging person?

6.   Do you threaten others?

7.   Do you deny your own problems and need for love?

8.   Do you believe that you can change your partner?

9.   Are you easily depressed?

10.   Do you find it hard to accept what happens to you?

co-dependent

FREEDOM LIST

Freedom from co-dependency is achievable. Here are some goals:

1. You will be able to think and talk about other things besides someone else's problems.

2. You won't feel the need to change other people's behavior.

3. You will see your role as an encourager, rather than a rescuer.

4. You will know when it's time to get out before it's too late.

5. You will be able to implement tough love, which actually demonstrates the most caring, and has boundaries in place.

Once you understand co-dependency and begin to accept that you aren't responsible for another person's actions and that you can't control the situation and don't hold the cure for the situation, you can then stop supporting someone else's bad habits and get on with developing a healthy life of your own.

A co-dependent relationship is one where the partners have difficulty being themselves while in a relationship. In any relationship, people tend to experience the battle between being themselves and being part of a relationship. In a healthy relationship, this can be dealt with openly; as a result, both partners can increasingly feel more secure in the relationship and more intimate as they grow as individuals.

In a co-dependent relationship, these issues are more difficult to deal with. Often they are simply swept under the rug or dealt with in an unhealthy atmosphere of accusations of selfishness, or one partner finds a way to intimidate the other. As a result, there is growing resentment within the relationship.

A co-dependent person may otherwise be known as a "rescuer" or "martyr" and they are usually attracted to people who need help, such as alcoholics, drug users, sex addicts, the mentally or physically ill and, perhaps most insidiously, selfish, irresponsible or ambitious people who need someone to support them while they look after their own interests.

Unfortunately, people who have co-dependent personalities usually do not see their own problems, nor do they see the need to take responsibility for them. They are only able to recognize their efforts to help others and they wonder why they are not celebrated or rewarded for them. They simply do not see the choices they have made.

Boundaries

When you have identified the key issues and you properly understand your own personal value, it is time to establish some necessary boundaries to protect the health of the relationships in your life. It is vitally important that you don't settle for less than the best for you. This may mean that you have to kiss the harmful and destructive relationships goodbye.

It may be that you will need to detach yourself from the other person and take responsibility for managing only your own life, and in the process, try to be kind to yourself. Detachment or distance from another person does not involve rejecting the actual person, it is simply rejecting the feeling of complete responsibility for them.

To become detached from another person requires us to understand who we are. Being able to detach involves having well-defined boundaries.

Sometimes we must make a choice that will require a severing of a relationship, if personal boundaries have been transgressed. Having clear boundaries is essential to a healthy, balanced lifestyle. A boundary is a personal property line that marks those things that we are responsible for. When we establish boundaries, we establish who we are and who we are not, where we want to go and where we do not want to go.

Relational naivety and deception can bring pain, and failure to establish adequate boundaries can leave a person feeling deceived, used, abused and afraid. An absence of boundaries allows us to be lulled into a false sense of security which in turn allows us to be led by our feelings and by flattery, which make us susceptible to the advances of someone who is setting out to take advantage of us.

That's why sexual boundaries are so important. Our self-esteem affects our attitudes towards sex. Our behavior reflects our self-esteem and our self-esteem is reflected in our behavior. A great sex life is experienced when people have identifiable boundaries in place to protect not just their body, but also their mind, will, emotions and heart.

Problems will arise when we fail to set good boundaries and maintain them and also when we bond to the wrong kind of people instead of the right kind of people. Outside of relationships, boundaries are easy to see. Fences, walls, signs, or hedges are all physical boundaries.

boundaries

In their book *Boundaries*, Dr. Henry Cloud and Dr. John Townsend write:

"Boundaries define us. They define what is me and what is not me. A boundary shows me where I end and someone else begins... Knowing what I am to own and take responsibility for gives me freedom. If I know where my yard begins and ends, I am free to do with it what I like... if I do not 'own' my life, my choices and options become very limited."

Within relationships, boundaries impact all areas of our lives:

★ Physical boundaries help us decide who may touch us and under what circumstances.

★ Mental boundaries give us the freedom to have our own thoughts and opinions. It's your right to have freedom of speech.

★ Emotional boundaries help us to deal with our own emotions, and to deflect the negative and manipulative emotions of others. It's your right to maintain unhindered feelings.

The primary purpose of any wall is for protection. Walls are there to keep vulnerable and valuable things in and harmful things out. However, walls that are built because of fear or negative experiences can isolate and contain you.

Some people learn early on in life that it is unsafe to get too close to others, particularly when someone they loved has hurt them. Once this defensive and self-protective belief is instilled, walls are built to protect that belief. The problem is that loneliness and isolation will become an unhealthy by-product.

Other people learn to believe early on in life that in order to be happy, they should have no boundaries at all. The problem with this extremity is that continual heartache and pain will become an unhealthy by-product of this kind of living.

Boundaries assist us to live in balance, providing that the boundaries we have in place resemble a fence with a gate rather than a brick wall. The fence means that we can see over it and that we can't hide behind it, and the gate enables us to come and go freely and others to come and go as we choose. What you don't want to build into your life is either a brick wall that says "keep out," or no fence at all that says "everyone welcome."

Conflict Management

When it comes to problems, we need to discover our role so that we can be empowered to make necessary changes. That's when we can either turn the situation around by our actions, perhaps even severing the relationship if appropriate. When we can't see our role in the problem, we lose our power and potentially stay trapped indefinitely.

We've been taught that relationships should be fifty-fifty. In other words, "You do your part, and I'll do mine." I have learned, however, that in order to build healthy, strong relationships we need to aim for a one hundred–one hundred ratio. Even if we fall short of this idea, there should be enough juice in the relationship tank to compensate. If we only agree to do what is minimal, we can expect disaster. If we agree and try to give a hundred percent, we can expect to flourish relationally.

I believe every person is responsible for the presence or absence of love. In any relationship, each person is constantly reacting to the other and we tend to react according to how we are treated. When you are accepted and appreciated by someone, you usually feel loved and automatically accept and appreciate that person in return. But when you are judged or criticized, you become upset, judgmental and critical in return. When we react, rather than respond, we are not taking responsibility for our own lives. If you are being mistreated, you are still able to respond constructively without becoming a doormat.

In his book *Love is Never Enough*, Dr. Aaron T. Beck analyzes actual dialogue to draw attention to the most common problems experienced by couples, including the power of negative thinking, disillusionment, rigid rules and expectations, and miscommunication.

When looking at the issue of miscommunication in conflict, Dr. Beck says, "Rather than seeing that there is a misunderstanding, conflicting partners misattribute the problem to the mate's "meanness" or "selfishness." Unaware that they are misreading their spouses, partners incorrectly ascribe base motives to them."

We can all get it wrong when we try to second-guess each other's motives and feelings and it's usually just a matter of time before someone gets hurt and upset. We put up walls of protection and resist, attack or withdraw. Then our partner may become upset and do the exact same thing in return and then we become even more upset and react more fiercely, and so the cycle of conflict goes on. The good news is that to create and maintain this cycle, there must be two people participating, meaning, if you refuse to attack or withdraw or react, then chances are the cycle will be broken and a fresh start can be made.

Once you discover your role in the conflict, you can do something about it. You can end the cycle of conflict and restore the love. Conflict management is the practice of identifying and handling conflict in a sensible, fair and efficient manner through effective communicating, problem solving and negotiating.

We need to live on the right side of "if". Instead of saying to ourselves, "If he apologizes first, then I will apologize," how about saying, "If I apologize, then at least I will have peace of heart and mind." Make the "if" relate to your actions, not your partner's. Living on the right side of "if" empowers us to live in freedom and to take responsibility for our own lives.

To handle conflict constructively, first you will need to make a decision that you will not attack your partner when you get angry. Decide that when there is a conflict between you, you will aim to resolve it as quickly and as constructively as possible.

Although difficulties in any relationship are normal, many relationships do survive such challenges, but healthy relationships are only built with commitment and effort. We can choose to just survive, or we can choose to thrive. It's the difference between existing and living, and it's our choice.

Mr. Wrong

At the age of sixteen I had my first "real" boyfriend. I thought he was the man of my dreams, but he turned out to be anything but. I chose not to listen to my parents and he hurt my feelings terribly, and I didn't see it coming. It seemed that everything I was taught as a child didn't relate to my life as a young woman. My parents hadn't brought me up to be hurt and discarded. They had brought me up in a home of love and respect, but I chose to throw it all away for what I thought was love.

What I shared with this guy was not love. He harassed me constantly about being too fat, even when I was so thin I looked sick. He often referred to my size and commented whenever I tried to eat anything. So, I wouldn't eat anything. He also reminded me constantly that he wished I was blonde, but I couldn't be thinner or blonde, it just wasn't me.

Eventually, I saw a glimpse of the future — of what my life should be like, could be like, would be like, if I could only be strong enough to walk away. And that's exactly what I did after years of hanging on. Once I freed myself from this damaging relationship, I could hold my chin up and start feeling human again.

healthy conflict

When conflict arises and you feel angry with your partner, try to follow these steps:

1. Admit that you are angry. Try using "I" statements to let your partner know how you are feeling, rather than "You" statements, which will be heard as an attack and lead the other person to be defensive, making the conflict even worse. However, admitting your anger is different from expressing it. Be strong, but don't shout and swear.

2. Ask for time out. This is essential if either you or your partner feels too angry to talk about the problem. Cooling down before discussing the issue is a good idea, but set a limit on it — don't use time out to avoid or ignore the issue indefinitely.

3. Check your feelings. There is nearly always another feeling underlying anger, like sadness, hurt or disappointment. Let your partner know how you feel. The underlying feeling will usually be a clue to the real issue that you and your partner need to face up to and talk about.

4. Listen to your partner's point of view. There may be an angle on the situation that you haven't considered.

5. Be prepared to acknowledge your part in the problem. Being willing to apologize does not mean that you are accepting all the responsibility.

6. Ask yourself what you can learn from the conflict. This will improve your relationship and lessen the chances of a similar conflict happening again.

7. Be prepared to forgive and make up as soon as possible. Don't make your partner wait as a punishment. Reunion after conflict can lead to a deepening of closeness and intimacy in the relationship.

Building Blocks

Acknowledging the existence of an unhealthy relationship is the first step to either restoring or ending it. Taking an inventory of the relationship and identifying the problem areas is the second step, and you may need professional help to do this properly.

For some people, the word "relationship" means security, happiness and peace, and for others it simply means shattered dreams and hell on earth.

Relationships come in all shapes and sizes, and every relationship is unique. The variations are seemingly infinite. If life were easy and predictable, here is how the perfect relationship might go:

★ You are on your own and feeling all right with yourself.
★ You meet someone you would like to get to know better.
★ The two of you decide to go out together.
★ You both have a really good time on your first date, when you discover what you have in common.
★ You go out again and your friendship and relationship grows.
★ After going out together several times you both realize you have found someone special.
★ You fall in love and continue to go out regularly.
★ You decide to get married.
★ You plan the wedding together and await the big day.
★ You get married.
★ You have 2.3 children.
★ You live happily ever after.

As you probably realize, life is rarely easy or predictable, so it doesn't always work out according to this list. There are many reasons why things often don't work out this way. This is because relationships and people can be very different. Not everyone wants the same type of relationship, nor do they want the same type of person.

This sounds obvious, but I think we don't acknowledge or accept when the person we love is the one who is disagreeing with us. This conflict within a relationship is not exclusive to those people who don't have it all together — it can happen to the "I've got it all together" people too. When partners view the relationship differently, it can cause endless inner turmoil and will be a key ingredient in an unhealthy relationship.

The good news is that even if you are in the midst of an unhealthy relationship, within every ounce of pain lies a ton of potential. For every bad choice, a good choice needs to be made. This requires action and effort. The past needs to be left behind and the future needs to be the focus. Life is full of choices. We are all born with a will, and with that will, we make a way for ourselves. We determine our way, the way in which we lead our lives, by our own choices. Choose to live and love.

As the saying goes, "You need to be cruel to be kind." Sometimes you just need to be what may seem cruel to what is hurting you, and kind to yourself. In order to be truly kind to yourself, you need to cut off destructive relationships, even though it seems like the hardest thing to do. This is the only way to free yourself up for your future because at the end of the day, freedom is what you crave and what you need. You deserve to be in a relationship that is totally healthy, totally committed, yet totally free.

Following are some practical building blocks to help you flourish regardless of your past:

1. Acknowledge that you are valuable.

2. Don't receive criticism and abuse.

3. Think carefully about whom you choose to start a relationship with.

4. Clearly communicate your wishes and respect the wishes of others.

5. Remember that you have the right to start again.

For those in destructive relationships, inside the depth of your pain lies the heart of your potential - the potential to rise up and get out of a situation you were never created to be in. Whether your pain is your fault or someone else's, it's within your power, through your will and your choice, to do something positive about it.

Many people unfortunately go looking for love in all the wrong places. This is all too common a problem. Boy meets girl, boy dumps girl, girl never gets over it!

Life may knock you down to the ground and knock the stuffing out of you, but it's never too late to get back up again. Good people get hurt and age has nothing to do with it. Relationship breakdown can happen at any time.

If you have made unwise decisions that have landed you in trouble, now is the time to do something positive with your future. Don't drag your pain into your future. The past is the past. You can't change it, no one can. Even if you are a victim of someone else's rotten behavior towards you, you can use it to empower your future. See their behavior as a lesson in what 'not to do', rise above the pain they inflicted on you by choosing to love and forgive, and this will make you stronger and in charge of your life. No matter what you've been through, remember, you are not a 'has been,' you are a 'will be'!

Determining what a healthy relationship should look like is a great place to start. A healthy relationship is based upon respect, when you can have fun together, when you both feel like you can be yourselves, when you can have different opinions and interests and when you listen to each other. Trust is another important factor, as is an absence of jealousy. Then, of course, there's compromise and the ability to apologize and talk disagreements through. Breathing space is also crucial. You don't have to spend all of your spare time together— you can spend time on your own, or with your own friends and family.

For a relationship to be healthy and for you to feel good about yourself, be the one to show goodwill by offering to make it work— don't wait for your partner. You may be pleasantly surprised by how much difference taking the first small step can make. Start with you.

Be supportive and don't make judgments when your partner makes mistakes or does things differently than you would do them. Ask for help when you cannot cope with a situation. Share the domestic load, offering to do what you like to do most, but being prepared to do whatever it takes for the job to be done. Allow yourself the right to put your feet up and relax and make time specifically for you — have a bath, read, listen to music, spend time with friends.

When you are able to express your feelings honestly and show appreciation to your partner for their contribution, when you listen to others and take responsibility for your own life, then you will begin to see healthy relationships develop and flourish in the future.

If you say "I love him," ask yourself the reasons why. Is he kind, considerate, caring? Is it real love or infatuation? Is it possible that what you think is love, is anything but? Only real love will last and it is not an illusion. Look for someone with the qualities you respect and admire. Being attracted to someone is important initially, but it doesn't mean you will stay attracted to them forever. Wise up and beware of unhealthy relationship traps.

"First-mile love" is primarily about chemistry and feelings, but "second-mile love" is more about construction, choice and commitment. On that note, I'll leave you with these words from Louis de Bernières's novel *Captain Corelli's Mandolin*: "Love itself is what is left over when being in love has burned away, and this is both an art and a fortunate accident."

Remember the Truth:
real love takes commitment.

healthy relationship check list

1.   You can both manage conflict and differences without despair or threats.

2.   You both protect and nourish the relationship and make it a priority.

3.   You both know how to be responsible for your own needs and also for the care of the relationship.

4.   You both feel 'special' to the other. Arguments or fights do not lead to abuse or threats.

5.   You both communicate wants, needs, feelings and emotional issues with little or no shame.

6.   There is unconditional love.

7.   The relationship feels and is nurturing, comfortable and fun.

8.   You respect each other physically.

9.   Both partners are honest.

10.   There is no abuse — physical, verbal or emotional.

10 keys to freedom
[from unhealthy relationships]

Forgiveness can be one of the hardest keys to freedom (see Chapter 9 for concrete suggestions on how to forgive). The following keys will help you remember that when you find yourself in, or heading towards, a relationship that is unhealthy, you can get FREE!

1. Forgive everyone who has hurt you in a relationship. This may take time, but commitment to the process will set you free.

2. Throw away things that remind you of pain in your past relationships.

3. Don't call or harass a former partner, as it will only damage your self-esteem even further.

4. See yourself as valuable and choose your relationships accordingly — the Prince/Princess is so much better than the Beast.

5. Try not to make the same mistake twice.

6. Walk away from an abusive relationship and get help from family or friends.

7. Lift your future standards higher than your past experiences.

8. Don't replace one dependency for another, such as relationships for drugs or alcohol.

9. Don't allow yourself to be pressured into sex.

10. Believe that you are someone special, on this earth for something special.

body & soul
[action plan]

Body

Never allow anyone to violate you physically. Ensure the necessary boundaries are in place so you don't get yourself into a situation where you feel pressured.

Soul

Release yourself from people who have hurt you in relationships, forgive quickly and learn to get on with the future without bringing up the past. Believe for the right life partner for you and the ability and strength to stay in love, well after the initial phase is over.

**My goal is Freedom
FROM UNHEALTHY RELATIONSHIPS**

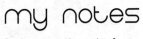

[write your thoughts]

chapter seven

Beneath Skin Deep

freedom from physical and mental challenges

["We are scarred by operations, by accidents, by war – by life …
Who turned our bravery into shame? Who told us scars are ugly?"]

beauty and the beast

Once upon a time a hard-working man fell on difficult times. His spoiled children didn't like going without, except for his youngest daughter, Beauty. She was willing and kind hearted.

Thankful for her unselfishness, Beauty's father decided to bring her a beautiful red rose. But while searching for the perfect bloom, he became lost in a blizzard. For hours he stumbled through the freezing forest until he found what seemed to be an old abandoned castle, where he took shelter. As he was leaving, he remembered the rose for Beauty. There were many beautiful red roses in the castle garden, so he picked one. Suddenly there was a loud noise and a man in a dark mask stood in his path.

"I did not give you the freedom to roam my castle! How dare you steal from me. I have a mind to kill you right now!" the angry man roared

Beauty's father begged for mercy and explained who the rose was intended for.

The masked man growled menacingly and said, "Your life will be saved if Beauty lives here with me. Go and bring her to me!"

Beauty's father left with a heavy heart. When he arrived home, Beauty learned of his experience with the masked man and insisted on going to the castle. When she and her father arrived, the masked man greeted them, but Beauty was barely able to look at him, not because of his mask, but because of his frightful manner. With many tears, Beauty kissed her father goodbye. Thus began Beauty's life in the castle. Each day she wandered through the many rooms and gardens, but met no one.

Beauty had always shown kindness towards people and she made an effort to befriend the masked man. He was her only hope for a friend and her affection for him began to grow. He earned his name, "Beast," because of his frightful temper, but Beauty discovered the masked man was actually kind and generous. One day he told her about a terrible accident that had caused his face to be disfigured, and she began to understand him. The more she came to know him, the more lovely he became in her sight. But she still missed her family.

The next evening, Beauty decided to ask if she could see her family just once more. The masked man wept, but he loved Beauty so much that he could deny her nothing. He sent her home with four chests of precious jewels, instructing her that she must return to him within two months, otherwise he would die.

When Beauty arrived home she fell into her father's embrace, overwhelmed to be home at last. Two months passed and Beauty remembered that the masked man would die if she didn't return. Immediately she dashed back to the castle. There she found him, lying in the grounds, nearly dead.

"Please wake up! Please don't die! I love you."

His heart began to beat as her very presence revived him.

"Beauty, have you come back to me?"

Removing his mask, Beauty replied, "Yes, I love you!" Her heart overflowed with love as she saw beyond his mask and his scars and into his heart. Beauty and the masked man married and enjoyed a lifetime of true love, and they both lived happily ever after.

the end

fact

Having a special need will require an ability to overcome extra challenges.

truth

People who have a special need can have as many joys and achievements as everyone else and are as beautiful as everyone else.

mirror mirror on the wall ...

why am I so different from them all?

This chapter is dedicated to some very courageous people whom I consider champions of self-esteem. These people have more reason than most to feel not so great about themselves, but they often surface with a healthier self-esteem and a more secure identity than many other people who have fewer challenges to overcome. There is much that we can learn about ourselves from taking a look at their lives. These people have had to learn how to live with the challenges of having a disfigurement or special needs, and with being judged on being different or on what they cannot do rather than what they can do.

There is no doubt that people who live with disfigurement or special needs have every opportunity to achieve as much and sometimes more in life, than those who have few struggles to overcome. Super achieving is not unknown territory for these people who choose to overcome. If someone says 'you can't' then these tenacious heroes say "yes I can."

This type of courage is a wonderful role model to people who don't have great self-esteem because it is based on overcoming challenges. I find the lives of others who may be disadvantaged to be an inspirational mirror, reflecting all that's both good and bad in life.

The aim of this chapter is to help us focus on seeing beneath skin-deep, to help you if you have special needs, to see beyond physical or mental limitations, regardless of whether you were born with a certain condition or found yourself disabled or disfigured later in life.

Special Needs

Having special needs basically means that a person is not able to do something that other people of their age and community can do, because of a physical or mental condition. It can affect every area of life: social, physical, emotional and mental. It can mean extra challenges and sometimes difficulties to overcome, but people who have special needs can also have as many joys and achievements as other people.

Many pictures may enter our mind when we think of the term "special needs." We may see the symbol of the stick figure in the wheelchair that shows where people with special needs can have access, or we may see a person with cerebral palsy, or perhaps a blind person with a guide dog. All these pictures do define special needs to a degree, but there are many more people affected by special needs than sometimes meets an able eye.

A special need can mean a number of different things:

★   An intellectual disability
★   A neurological or learning disability
★   A physical disfigurement
★   A physical disability
★   The presence in the body of a disease-causing organism (such as HIV)
★   A psychiatric disability
★   A sensory disability

Disability is a loss of physical or mental function, for example, a person who has quadriplegia, a brain injury, epilepsy or a vision or hearing impairment. It also means loss of part of the body, such as in the case of amputation. Then there is malfunction, malformation or disfigurement of a part of a person's body, which may be caused by diabetes, asthma, birthmarks or scars.

A person who may learn differently from other people, such as a person suffering from dyslexia, has a disability. Any condition that affects a person's thought process, understanding of reality, emotions or judgment, or which results in disturbed behavior, for example mental illness, depression, neurosis or personality disorder, is a disability.

We now refer to these as "special needs" as it more correctly defines them. People with these attributes are not disabled, meaning "unable," they merely have special requirements in order to achieve what some of us find easier. They are not unable to achieve — they just take another pathway to achieving.

There are obviously particular challenges that people with special needs face in their social lives. They may find it particularly hard to have high self-esteem and to feel good about themselves. This is where good friendships help. Friendships should be a source of emotional support and good friendships should be enriching, involve a sharing of common interests, and be fun. Basically, friends should make life more enjoyable. Good friends are vital and can definitely help with having a healthy self-esteem.

The journey to discovering their value can be long and painful for people with physical needs, and there are several reasons for this. People who are diagnosed as "special" at birth or early in childhood may have parents who expected that they would be "normal" and independent in their adult lives and so their rejection can be a significant hindrance to a healthy self-esteem.

Parents of special needs children could also be overprotective and thus encourage the child to become co-dependent. These attitudes and behaviors do not help a child with special needs to build a healthy and strong self-esteem and sense of identity.

For people who find themselves with special needs in adulthood, it is often the realization of their worst nightmare. We all grow up with the stereotype that people with special needs are a burden to their families, they are different and life is just so awkward for them. We sat on the other side of the fence and when suddenly you are thrust into the arena of special needs, all those stereotypes come back to haunt you and you may eventually accept them as your reality. Our self-esteem needs to be shaped by our value as people, and not by any special need that we may be living with.

If you have a special need, you may have experienced some of the following things and they may have damaged your self-esteem:

★ Being constantly put down or humiliated at home, work, school or anywhere
★ Being expected to take the blame for things that are not your fault or are out of your control
★ Not having your emotional, social or physical needs met
★ Being abused in some way, for example, physical or emotional abuse
★ Being harassed or discriminated against because of the way you look, walk or talk
★ Being labeled by other people as disabled

★ Being subjected to strong messages from the media or the community about what you are expected to be like.

Living in a culture that gives an unrealistic definition of what is "perfect" and then expects us to strive towards that perfection, can definitely cause you to question whether or not you fit in, and in turn can affect how you feel about yourself. Definitions are important, but labels can be damaging for the individual when they are misused, and they are misused in a variety of ways.

In defining a person's special need, it's vitally important we don't use labels that may dehumanize or devalue or rob dignity from an individual, making the physical or intellectual condition the focus of their life, rather than the person themselves. If we look beyond our own personal experiences and environments, we'll understand there is not a "one-size-fits-all" definition of special needs.

Beauty and the Beast

In my version of the story *Beauty and the Beast*, we read that the man regarded as the Beast gained this name not only because of his looks but because of his temper. The Beast had learned to live with his disfigurement hidden behind a mask. He lived marginalized and alienated by others, and he was terribly unhappy. When people are disfigured, some people have difficulty seeing past their outward appearance. This in turn causes people who have already suffered enough to have to put up with people's reaction of revulsion and fear.

Beauty, on the other hand, was beautiful not just because of the way she looked, but because of her kind heart and her willingness to accept and embrace the Beast exactly as he was.

Life isn't simple or perfect. It sometimes throws us curve balls and we need to learn to deal with them. We spend so much energy trying to dodge the curve balls, maybe we should teach ourselves to catch them! That's what I believe people with special needs often do: they don't dodge the curve balls — they learn to catch them.

True Champions

Professional surfer Bethany Hamilton is a true champion! On October 31, 2003, Bethany was surfing off the coast of Hawaii when she was attacked by a 14-foot tiger shark, who nearly ate her for lunch.

Bethany escaped with her life, and her friends assisted her back to shore, but not before the shark bit off her left arm. While Bethany may have lost her arm, she gained international celebrity from the attack. More importantly, she got back on her surfboard just four months after the shark attack and placed fifth in her age group at the National Surfing Championships. Since the attack, Bethany has won multiple surfing contests and won the ESPY Award for Best Comeback Athlete.

Bethany Hamilton hasn't let a savage shark attack end her dream of becoming a surfer. She says she has to kick a lot harder to make up for the loss of her arm but she still loves surfing as much as ever. She's painted a special pattern on her surfboard that helps ward off sharks and she no longer goes surfing during the early morning -- a shark's favorite feeding time. Bethany has also used her new-found influence to inspire others and help charitable causes.

Nick Vujicic was born with no arms no and no legs. Growing up, Nick dealt with many issues such as bullying, depression and loneliness. Needless to say, Nick struggled greatly with self-esteem.

He did not understand why he was different from everyone else and constantly questioned the purpose of his life, if there was one at all. Encouragement from his friends and family, paired with a supportive upbringing allowed Nick to grow confident in himself. With this confidence, he found the purpose he was searching for.

Starting at the age of 19, Nick began travelling the world sharing his story with vast demographics including youth, businessmen, and entrepreneurs. His story has encouraged and inspired millions of people around the world to see the purpose in their own lives and to live life to the fullest. Despite what may have seemed to be a drawback to society, Nick chose to allow his disability to move not only his life forward, but also the lives of those around him as well.

Thank goodness that in the twenty-first century, people like Bethany and Nick can achieve and succeed just like everyone else.

Generations ago, this wasn't the story.

Joseph Merrick, otherwise known as the "Elephant Man," was born in England in 1862. Joseph first began to develop tumors on his face before his second birthday. His physical condition worsened as bulbous, cauliflower-like growths developed on his head and body, and his right hand and forearm became a useless club.

Even so, Joseph had a wonderful imagination. Unfortunately, for much of his life his imagination was all he had. Even though he was highly intelligent (and self-educated), he was never accepted socially because of his appearance. He had to rely mostly upon his imagination.

It was said of Joseph in a letter to *The Times* newspaper in December 1886, "Women and nervous persons fly in terror from the sight of him, and...he is debarred from seeking to earn a livelihood in any ordinary way, yet he is superior in intelligence, can read and write, is quiet, gentle, not to say even refined in his mind."

Later in life, Joseph was unable to get a job; he lived destitute and stripped of all his self-worth by the ignorant people of the day. He was prepared to take any job that would offer him a living. As a last resort he took a job as a sideshow 'freak.' He died having never known the freedom of life as we know it. He was a prisoner within his disability, because of the ignorance of people who did not know what to do with him.

Seeing the movie *The Elephant Man* as a teenager had a profound impact on me - I have never been the same since. I view all people, regardless of their physical or mental condition, as equal. I may be different, but I am not worth less than anyone else. I believe *The Elephant Man* taught me a lesson in life that I couldn't have learned without hearing this wonderful and courageous story.

Other stories have had a similar impact on me. I have great memories of my kindergarten school days, when I made my first friends. One of them was a boy named Mark and he was very special. Mark was born with no legs and only half an arm, but he was a champion soccer player and one of the most popular kids at school. He lived like a champion and inspired everyone around him.

Brett is another wonderful person whom I have had the privilege of getting to know. Brett has cerebral palsy, but he is by no means unable to live a wonderful and fulfilled life. When I first met Brett at sixteen, he was in a wheelchair, but he soon progressed to walking braces and then very trendy wooden canes. I can remember going on a youth group camping trip with a bunch of young people, including Brett. When it came to chores, Brett was in there with the rest of us. When it came to sleeping on a mattress on the floor of a tent, he was in that too. Brett got his driver's license and a fantastic job in computing and he was a major contributor to the lives of young people in our youth group.

There was no stopping this inspiring young guy. The only things that occasionally got in his way, were his legs! And he used to get over his legs not working by cracking jokes about them and making everyone feel at ease. Brett realized that the 'able' folk were having more trouble adjusting than he was. Brett is now happily married and is spending his life helping others build theirs. His attitude and outlook on life are amazing!

The way that we respond to those who have a special need directly reflects our own level of self-esteem. How do you feel when you encounter someone who has a special need or who is disfigured? Are you uncomfortable, embarrassed or unsure? Just remember, if you are overcome with these feelings, then this is all about you and not them!

Scars of Life

Our skin is a diary of our experiences, changing as we age. Its layers are a record of our past, of our pain and our joys, and of today as it slides into memory. Scraped knees from fights in the playground, chicken pox scars from the one spot that we just had to scratch. Bruises and scars. Wrinkles from all the smiling and laughing we have done. Every mark is a groove in the record of our life. We all know that we have physical skin to deal with, but we also have emotional skin to deal with, and that too can be scarred.

We are scarred by operations, by accidents, by war — by life. Women may be scarred by the miracle of birth, and I have my fair share of stretch marks to prove it! I have chosen to see these scars as 'love tattoos' rather than unsightly and unacceptable marks. I am proud of them as they represent the lives of my beautiful children. These symbols become a rite of passage in life. So why is it then that to many, scars cause feelings of fear instead of being seen as the badges of courage and honor that they truly are? Who turned our bravery into shame? Who told us scars are ugly? And why do so many of us believe it?

The fact is, a person with no special need can have very low self-esteem and someone with a severe special need may have very high self-esteem. Although we all feel better about ourselves if we are 'looking good', true self-esteem is not linked directly to appearance. However, the psychological consequences (or scars) of having a special need or being disfigured are very real.

The great news is that many people with special needs are triumphant over all the bombardment of negativity. They are living lives of fulfillment and are active, contributing members of their communities.

Taking Control

You can't change other people, but what you can do is change the way you see yourself. You can nurture and look after yourself. You also have control over the way you think, feel or behave in your life, regardless of whether you have a special need or not.

It is vital that you are true to yourself. You will never be able to make everyone happy or meet everyone's expectations about how they think you should be, but you can make yourself happy.

If you have a special need, your self-esteem may be positive or negative, but it is not set in concrete. It can always grow and it can always be improved. If your self-esteem is low, then there are things you can do to boost how you see yourself. When someone has a healthy or more positive self-esteem, they are able to accept themselves. This means acknowledging that we all have strengths and weaknesses, and the weaknesses are absolutely fine, as are the strengths. A healthy or positive self-esteem does not mean that someone has an inflated or self-righteous view of themselves, it is having a balanced view — not over-emphasizing the strengths or weaknesses.

healthy self-esteem

There are many ways you can bring healthy self-esteem into your life. Here are some ideas for you to think about. You might use them all or choose the ones you think are best for you:

1. Be kind to yourself! Begin to appreciate yourself as a unique individual, and don't compare yourself with others.

2. Dream about what you would like for your life.

3. Challenge yourself to become more assertive.

4. Concentrate on your best qualities, then make a list of ways you might use these qualities in the future.

5. Give yourself permission to try and to fail.

6. Get involved in a sports team or join a community group that will help you give something back to others.

7. Do things that you enjoy and you know you are good at.

8. Help people work out how to respond to you.

9. Smile and accept compliments that come your way.

10. Take control of your life and you will feel better about   yourself.

It is good to remember that a special need is only one aspect of a person's life. For a person who has a special need, it is important for you to allow yourself to view your need as one component of many in your life — not the only component. Another issue you may be dealing with is discrimination and stereotypes from society.

Our society places emphasis on looks, ability and being the same as everyone else. This may make you feel additional pressure to try to meet society's impossible standards. Don't be sucked in by this pressure — whether you have a special need or not, we all feel the pressure to conform to these ideals of perfection and trying to only leaves us feeling less perfect and sometimes less human. Parents and friends may also have shaped your self-image and therefore affected your identity in ways you wish to change.

Renewing Your Mind

There are patterns of thinking that people with lower self-esteem may engage in more than people with higher self-esteem. These thinking patterns often result in a lack of confidence in either one, or many areas. A lack of confidence does not necessarily equal lack of ability. It may just be a false set of beliefs about yourself. For instance, you may believe you are not very smart, or are unable to play certain sports because of your physical attributes. Just because you were told this, doesn't mean it is true!

By acknowledging and changing some of these incorrect thinking patterns, you can begin to change how you view yourself. You may feel as though you have had to become an expert at playing on a field that is not level as a result of dealing with your special need and people's attitudes towards it. You need to address not only how you play the game, but the part you play as well. Don't settle for playing the pawn if you could play the queen or king.

To help you do this, you need to maximize your positive abilities and minimize your limitations, and remember that everyone has limitations, whether they have a special need or not. You should also avoid unrealistic comparisons, and when you are setting goals, make them realistic for your own life.

Another important thing to remember is to try not to overemphasize your special need. There is more that you can do than you probably realize. There is a phenomenal woman — Joni Eareckson Tada — who was once an outgoing, athletic teenager.

One day at a picnic with her friends, she dove into a shallow river and broke her neck, becoming a quadriplegic. Reading her autobiography and seeing the movie based on her experiences literally changed my life. I realized how precious life is and that what happened to Joni could happen to anyone.

Joni firstly had to acknowledge her limitations, but then she learned to focus on her potential, and although she can't move her arms or her legs at all, she is a brilliant artist (having learned to paint using her mouth), a prolific writer and an excellent speaker. Joni is the epitome of "can do." Joni cried out, "If I can't die, then show me how to live." The trauma of a broken neck and the anguish of a hopeless future grabbed this seventeen-year-old girl's attention and started her on a new journey of learning to appreciate herself all over again.

Since then, she has written a number of books and had a movie made about her amazing capacity to overcome her needs in life. She now travels the world sharing her story and empowering people — special needs or no special needs. Joni learned how to take control of her life and understand who she truly is.

If you have suffered from a tragic accident as Joni did, you must re-learn to appreciate yourself — all of yourself. This means coming to terms with your needs too. There may be times when you feel completely frustrated, but try to focus on the positive aspects of your need. One way to do this is making a list of your strengths including how your need, or your method of dealing with it, is an asset. Think bigger than yourself — it may be something that you use to help others.

Privileged

I have the wonderful privilege of being step mom to a beautiful young man called Joshua. Joshua is my husband's son from his previous marriage, and he has special physical and intellectual needs. Joshua was diagnosed with cerebral palsy. He was born with the umbilical cord wrapped tightly around his neck. This tragically caused brain damage at birth and he has never recovered.

Christmas day at our place is always fun. We have a large family — six children (including Joshua), my parents, my grandmother, my sister and my niece. My beautiful grandmother had a stroke seven years before she passed away, and she had special needs of her own. When it came to sitting around the dinner table and enjoying Christmas dinner, our small (at the time) children learned how to respond to their grandmother who couldn't feed herself, and to Joshua who not only couldn't feed himself, but really enjoyed flinging food around the place!

Rather than feeling the need to shelter the smaller children from what could be seen as rather anti-social behavior, I helped them see how very special their grandmother and big brother were. They are learning at a young age to not just "tolerate" those who are different because of a special need, but to genuinely care for, learn from and enjoy the company of these very special family members of ours. I have often wondered what it would have been like to have actually given birth to Joshua myself. The first question any new parent wants to know is, "Is my baby okay?"

I know my husband, Jonathan, and Joshua's mother were devastated on learning of his need. My husband has talked to me about sometimes having to fight off feelings of inadequacy, as he faced the fact he couldn't change Joshua's condition. He came to terms with it and has learned to live way, way above what happened and because of that, is a wonderful father not only to Joshua, but to all of our children. He has determined not to allow what happened to rob his life or the life of his family.

We once took Joshua shopping to buy him some new shoes. He sat down while Jonathan and I went looking for sizes and styles of sneakers and when we returned, Joshua had taken off and we couldn't find him. Jonathan and I went up and down every aisle until we heard an extremely loud and excited shriek! It was Joshua! A lady standing next to me jumped with fright. I just turned to the woman and said, "I guess some people enjoy shopping more than others!"

Sometimes the hardest thing to deal with is helping other people understand that everything's okay.

True Beauty

Some people view their physical appearance, whether beautiful or not, as a limitation or a hindrance. Beautiful Hollywood movie star Audrey Hepburn had every reason to focus on outward appearance, but she chose to focus on a deeper sense of beauty — beauty from within. On the Christmas before she died, she read to her children a poem by Samuel Levenson called "Time Tested Beauty." These powerful words resound: "The beauty of a woman must be seen from in her eyes ... and is reflected in her soul." The real you, the beauty of you, is found in you and will shine through when you discover the truth of these words.

For others, living with a special need is like living trapped in a castle, hoping someone will discover the hidden treasure of the true you. Helen Keller once said, "The best and most beautiful things in the world cannot be seen or even touched. They must be felt with the heart."

We can learn much about beauty when we look at legends in history who have made a beautiful life from very unpleasant circumstances. People come in all shapes, sizes and colors — and real life cannot be airbrushed! Not all of us walk tall, or walk at all. Not all of us have perfect limbs or even have the use of all four.

Whether you feel that your life relates to the Beast's life or Beauty's life, there is something in this story for everyone to learn. We need to learn to love unconditionally; we also need to learn to allow ourselves to be loved unconditionally and to love ourselves unconditionally.

For those who have eyes to see, your inner beauty can be seen as a diamond. What makes you sparkle as a diamond is much more than your cut, color, clarity, and carat-weight. It's the combination of all these that give you your uniqueness, which is indefinable and immeasurable. It's what makes you completely unique — one in six billion!

A diamond is a brilliant, precious and very durable stone. Even if you are feeling like a lump of coal, this is the first stage of becoming a diamond. You need to know that at the very core of your being is brilliance, preciousness and durability.

You are a diamond waiting to be liberated, so that your greatness and true beauty can be revealed.

We are sometimes placed in circumstances that increase pressures in our lives until we too are changed from coal to a diamond. When you're going through tough times and tough experiences, just think — this is part of the process of making you shine even brighter.

Never forget what's inside you is more precious than you could ever imagine. Let your inner beauty shine. And it's only through healthy self-esteem this truly happens.

Your self-esteem is a direct reflection of how you feel about yourself, so grow to love who you are. Whether you have a special need or not, your life is what you make of it.

Remember the Truth:
people who have a special need can have as many
joys and achievements as everybody else
and are as beautiful as everyone else.

time tested
beauty tips

For attractive lips, speak words of kindness.
For lovely eyes, seek out the good in people.
For a slim figure, share your food with the hungry.
For beautiful hair, let a child run their fingers through it once a day.
For poise, move with the knowledge that you'll never walk alone.
People, even more than things, have to be restored, renewed, revived,
reclaimed and redeemed and redeemed and redeemed.
Never throw out anybody.
Remember, if you ever need a helping hand, you'll find one at the end
of your arm.
As you grow older you will discover that you have two hands.
One for helping yourself, the other for helping others.
The beauty of a woman is not in the clothes she wears, the figure that
she carries, or the way she combs her hair.
The beauty of a woman must be seen from in her eyes, because that
is the doorway to her heart, the place where love resides.
The beauty of a woman is not in a facial mole, but true beauty in a
woman is reflected in her soul.
It is the caring that she lovingly gives, the passion that she knows.
And the beauty of a woman, with passing years only grows!

SAMUEL LEVENSON

10 keys to freedom
[from physical and mental challenges]

FREEDOM is a journey as well as a fulfillment of your heart's desire. These keys will help you to practice taking your gaze away from the challenges you face. Start making changes for the better and watch everyone else catch up!

1.   Always hold your head high, and remember to smile!

2.   Remember, your adversity is also your opportunity.

3.   Discover and nurture that which is beautiful in you.

4.   Tell yourself and someone else every day that you and they are remarkable.

5.   Always say "thank you" when someone says something positive about you.

6.   Spend time as much time each day developing your internal beauty as you do in your external beauty.

7.   Appreciate the amazing world in which you live.

8.   Practice generosity daily by using your resources, abilities and creativity to help others.

9.   Remember that gracious behavior reflects a loving person, so work on becoming more gracious.

10.   As you grow older, remember that true beauty never fades with age, it only increases.

body & soul

[action plan]

Body

Hold your head up and please don't hide behind a mask. Self-acceptance and others' acceptance will tend to flow more freely as you refuse to allow fear to force you to hide.

Soul

You are more than your need. Tell yourself every single day that you are an outstanding human being, full of incredible potential, with the ability to be whoever you put your heart and mind to. Believe for healing and at the same time, believe for the ability to accept that which you cannot change and know that this is not what defines who you truly are.

My goal is Freedom
FROM PHYSICAL AND MENTAL
CHALLENGES

my notes

[write your thoughts]

chapter eight

The Balancing Act

freedom from eating disorders & extreme behavior
["Like any addiction, the beginnings of an eating disorder
start with a thought, and that thought is usually a lie which,
if entertained, becomes reality."]

goldilocks

Once upon a time, three bears lived happily together in a house in the woods. One bear was naturally thin, one was naturally athletic, and the third was naturally curvaceous.

The three bears loved to eat. There was a small bowl for the slim bear, a medium-sized bowl for the medium-sized bear and a larger bowl for the curvy bear. Even though their bowls were different sizes, the three bears ate about the same amount of food.

One day, as they were waiting for their oatmeal to cool, they decided to take a walk in the woods. While they were away, a young woman called Goldilocks came across their house. Seeing no one home, she let herself in.

Goldilocks didn't like her life at all. She had a lovely figure, similar to that of the curvy bear, but she couldn't see that she was beautiful. She was troubled and had been starving herself for weeks, so now she couldn't resist the oatmeal that lay steaming on the table.

Goldilocks tried the first bowl, but it was too hot, then she tried the next bowl, but it was too cold. The last bowl was just right, so she gobbled it up. But not being able to stop at just one bowl, Goldilocks devoured the other two bowls too.

Then she headed for the pantry, the refrigerator and the freezer to see what other food she could find. She found plenty more including bread, cheese, chocolate and ice cream. She ate all of it, and looked for more. Goldilocks was completely out of control. With so much food in her stomach Goldilocks felt sick, so she made herself throw up. Then she just wanted to lie down and sleep. Trapped in a downward spiral she felt guilty and ashamed, so she sobbed herself to sleep upstairs on one of the bears' beds.

After a while the three bears came home to eat their breakfast, but all they saw were three empty bowls.

"Somebody's been eating our oatmeal!" they exclaimed.

They began to look around the house. The curvy bear noticed that someone had been in the pantry, because all the food was gone. The athletic bear noticed that someone had been in the bathroom because the bathroom scales were left out.

Then the three bears went upstairs to look in the bedroom.

"There's someone in my bed!" cried the thin bear.

It was Goldilocks, who awoke with a fright and tried to run away because she knew she had been caught. But the bears stopped her.

They gently told Goldilocks not to be afraid and that she was welcome in their home because they wanted to help her.

Goldilocks told the bears how unhappy she was. She felt so sick and so ashamed. Wanting to help her, the kindly bears told her the truth and encouraged her not to hurt herself any more. The bears encouraged Goldilocks as they stood her in front of their mirror until she began to see the truth.

She knew it would take some time for her to be completely well again, but this moment of revelation had made her really consider what she had been doing.

Day by day, Goldilocks learned to appreciate who she was, to feel better about herself and to begin to live happily ever after.

the end

fact

Eating disorders can destroy your life, and extreme behavior will never build your life.

truth

Eating disorders and other extreme behavior can be overcome, and healthy balance can be achieved.

mirror mirror on the wall ...

why am I so unbalanced in it all?

Our lives can so easily get out of balance when we focus too heavily on any one aspect of our life, whether it's something physical, mental, emotional or relational. Obsessing over any one aspect of ourselves can lead us into a downward spiral of extreme behavior, as we begin to neglect or disregard other important areas of our life. Sometimes the pain we find ourselves in can lead us to find relief in ways that actually cause us further harm.

Extreme and self-destructive behavior can be seen in many different forms, such as an eating disorder, addiction to a substance or activity, self-harm or compulsions.

Eating Disorders

Eating disorders seem to be a socially acceptable way we can hurt ourselves in the twenty-first century. Drugs, excessive alcohol, smoking — we all know these are unacceptable, but starving yourself or eating and throwing up seems to be acceptable because many people do it and most of them not only get away with it, they are sometimes celebrated.

When I think about the insidious nature of eating disorders, I get really mad. It all starts with a lie; a lie that says "you can be in control if you do this", or "no one will know", or "you will be so beautiful if you do this". These lies are all utter nonsense. That's why it's so important to challenge your thought processes so you don't just accept everything you hear or that comes into your head.

Sadly, many people (especially young women) are driven either to starve themselves or compulsively eat against their own will. This is a result of a number of factors, such as personality type, family dynamics or background. Each of these things plays a significant part and people are affected to differing degrees. Regardless of the reason, our society is faced with a major health issue that has devastating effects, both physical and emotional, and can be fatal.

Many people can relate to not liking who they are or how they look and feeling as though no one understands them. We can sometimes tend to be controlling, yet completely out of control, and all we want is to be free. Every time we look in the mirror, our reflection is distorted in our own eyes and we go to great lengths to change our appearance to try to fit in.

Anorexia and Bulimia

The average starting age for females with eating disorders is approximately eleven years of age. Eating disorders are increasing in today's society and not just among teenage girls. The pressure that leads to a person developing an eating disorder doesn't discriminate according to gender or age. The onset of anorexia, bulimia and compulsive eating can occur at any time in a person's life.

Even though the reasons for the development of an eating disorder may vary, the self-perceptions are usually the same: self-hate, worthlessness and low self-esteem. Usually the person believes that thinness equals happiness. Some people may feel their life is out of control and so they focus in on an area of their life they can control — their weight. Others may believe that once they attain the perfect body image, their life will become ideal.

We can become prisoners of food. The very thing that we try to deny ourselves in order to be thin is the same thing that we use to hurt ourselves. Self-inflicted pain isn't always intentional and a sense of failure continues to feed the disease. This is the roller coaster of destruction that those who suffer from eating disorders are desperate to get off.

In her book *The Monster Within*, Cynthia Rowland McClure describes her life of torment as she struggled with an eating disorder she refers to in her book as 'her monster'. The book describes a conversation she had with herself about destructive behavior. She knew she was hurting herself, but she couldn't seem to stop. The monster of her own mind kept telling her how useless and worthless she was and that she wouldn't ever be able to stop.

The two main forms of eating disorders are anorexia nervosa and bulimia nervosa. Both of these illnesses have similar features, including a preoccupation with weight and food.

Anorexia is thought to affect one out of every two hundred women. It is twenty times more common in girls than boys. The affected person usually loses at least one-sixth of their body weight and sometimes much more. This happens because they refuse to eat enough food, despite feeling hungry.

A person suffering from anorexia usually has a false impression of their body size, believing they are fat when others say this is clearly not true. They have an intense fear of becoming fat and may obsessively collect diet or recipe books and other information about food and nutrition. They will often spend large amounts of time preparing food for others to eat.

Bulimia usually occurs in slightly older people, from the late teens onwards, and is more common than anorexia nervosa. It is believed that two to three in every one hundred women experience this problem. Many people suffering from bulimia will have had previous episodes of anorexia.

People with bulimia go on regular eating binges during which they consume large amounts of high-calorie food, usually in secret and much more rapidly than normal. During the binge they feel out of control and experience a loss of self-respect. To compensate, they make themselves vomit or use laxatives, enemas and diuretics or a combination of these methods to get rid of the weight they may have gained. They may also exercise obsessively. Often they are not underweight and so their problem is not as obvious as that of people with anorexia.

Several factors may be responsible for these illnesses. The media and fashion industries tend to portray thin women as the most attractive and teenagers naturally listen to these messages. Other possible factors that can contribute include personal issues such as poor self-image, insecurity, abuse, family problems, the fight for independence and even the pressure to be a high achiever. There are also genetic factors such as chemical imbalance or hormonal changes that can be compounded by stress or trauma, accompanied by a lack of adequate coping skills.

Goldilocks

By applying a new twist to a well known and loved fairy-tale, we see Goldilocks in a downward spiral, completely miserable with her life. In this adaptation, Goldilocks suffered from an eating disorder and her self-destructive behavior caused her to live with unbearable guilt and shame.

Sneaky and secretive behavior meant that she isolated herself and had no way of even being able to gauge the damage she was doing to herself. To support her destructive habits, Goldilocks stole from the three bears. She stole any food she could find: oatmeal, bread, blocks of cheese, tubs of ice cream — anything that would help feed the habit. And to punish herself for being such a "bad girl", Goldilocks vomited until she nearly passed out — full of overwhelming discontentment.

Goldilocks' story is one that could be told in countless households around the world. Anorexia, bulimia and binge eating (which is like bulimia except that the person doesn't try to get rid of the food after eating) are disorders that have drained the lives of millions of young people and the incidence of these disorders continues to increase in epidemic proportions.

It wasn't until Goldilocks was brought in front of and faced the mirror of truth that she was able to find true freedom.

Cause and Effect

It is widely understood that teenagers are under a lot of pressure to fit in and succeed. Many spend a great deal of time worrying about what others think and desperately try to conform to an unattainable body image: if they look a certain way, they will be accepted. Since many teenagers regularly buy teen or fashion magazines and watch movies and television shows featuring underweight models and actors, this only reinforces their belief that in order to be happy, successful and accepted, they must be thin.

Research has shown that the family environment can also play a big role in the development of teenage eating disorders. Being part of a family in which emotional, physical or sexual abuse is taking place, a teenager (or any person) may develop an eating disorder to gain a sense of control, to block out painful feelings and emotions or as a way to punish themselves — especially if they blame themselves for the abuse.

Most people with eating disorders will try to avoid conflict at all costs, so they usually don't express negative feelings. Instead, they try to wear a happy face all the time to try to please people. They end up using food as a way to stuff down all those negative feelings and purging usually gives them a sense of relief, almost as if they are releasing the built-up emotions.

Some teenagers are raised in families that are suffocating or don't allow any independence, and they may develop an eating disorder as a way to gain an identity for themselves. While a family that is close and in which people can talk to each other about their problems is great, being too close is not healthy, as teenagers need to develop their own identity within their family.

Being raised in a home where the parents are very weight conscious could lead the teenager to believe that weight and appearance are very important. Many teenage girls learn to diet by watching their mothers. Instead of learning that it is what's on the inside of a person that matters, they learn that appearance and looking good is the most important part of being a woman.

Eating disorders can be very much about control, so if a person feels as though everything around them is out of control, they may develop an eating disorder to regain some sense of control. It is important for families to raise their teenagers to be proud of who they are and not place undue importance on their appearance.

Warning, Warning

It wasn't until the 1980s that anorexia nervosa was recognized and diagnosed and since that time, its victims have grown in number and reduced in age.

On 4 February 1983, singer Karen Carpenter died at the age of thirty-two of heart failure caused by chronic anorexia nervosa. Karen's band, The Carpenters, was one of the most popular groups in history, selling nearly one hundred million records worldwide to date.

Karen had battled with anorexia nervosa for eight years after she was advised to lose a little weight. Six years into her battle, she was treated by a psychiatrist, but the damage had already been done. She remained obsessed and trapped by the disease.

Karen's case was extreme and she fought to overcome anorexia throughout the last two years of her life, but she just seemed to run out of time. Her body couldn't take any more. She had been starving herself for seven years using laxatives, drinking water with lemon, taking dozens of thyroid pills daily and even throwing up, and no amount of fame and fortune was enough to save her life.

There is no doubt that both anorexia and bulimia can have serious and even fatal consequences. Inadequate nutrition can cause problems with most parts of the body including kidney failure, muscle cramps and bladder and bowel problems. The recurrent vomiting of people with bulimia may damage the mouth, throat and stomach, and many girls with anorexia find that their periods stop and fine, downy hair may grow on all parts of their body.

Some specific medical problems associated with anorexia nervosa apart from the risk of death are:
★ Heart disease
★ Unhealthy cholesterol levels
★ Reproductive and hormonal abnormalities
★ Retarded growth in children and adolescents
★ Low birth weights, frequent miscarriages, and birth defects
★ Osteoporosis and other bone loss issues
★ Blood problems, including anemia
★ Gastrointestinal problems
★ Electrolyte imbalances
★ Bloating and constipation.

As well as physical problems, there may be marked personality changes including withdrawal from friendships, depression and mood swings. The chemical imbalances in the body may make clear thinking difficult, with obvious effects on work or study.

Some specific medical problems associated with bulimia include:
★ Tooth erosion, cavities and gum problems
★ Water retention, swelling and abdominal bloating
★ Loss of fluid
★ Low potassium levels, which can cause extreme weakness and near paralysis (this can be reversed when potassium is given). Dangerously low levels of potassium can result in lethal heart rhythms.

Help!

If you think you have an eating disorder, tell someone who can assist you in finding help. Do not feel that you are alone. There are people who love and care for you. Contact the eating disorder association in your city, or your local doctor, counselor, community health center or pastor. It is vital that if you have an eating disorder, you receive treatment from a qualified health professional.

Eating disorders can be treated and a healthy weight restored. The sooner these disorders are diagnosed and treated, the better the outcomes are likely to be. The first stage in accessing treatment is talking to a doctor. Most cases of anorexia nervosa or bulimia will require referral to a specialist, usually a psychiatrist or psychologist.

Most treatments can be managed through outpatient care but sometimes it is necessary to go into the hospital.

Treatment of anorexia calls for a specific program that involves three main phases:
1. Restoring the weight lost
2. Treating psychological disturbances such as distortion of body image, low self-esteem and interpersonal conflicts
3. Achieving long-term rehabilitation or full recovery

The primary goal of treatment for bulimia is to reduce or eliminate binge eating and purging behavior by establishing a pattern of regular, non-binge meals. Attitudes relating to the eating disorder need to be challenged and improved, as well as encouraging healthy but not excessive exercise.

Drug treatments can sometimes be useful in bulimia, but are rarely enough to stop the disorder. Restoring a normal body weight is necessary but not the only thing that will cure the problem. Psychological and physical issues need to be addressed together and this may involve cognitive behavioral therapy or family therapy. The treatment goals and strategies for binge-eating disorder are similar to those for bulimia.

It is important to realize that people with eating disorders often do not recognize or admit they are sick. As a result, they may strongly resist getting or staying in treatment, or both. Trust is a big issue. Family members or other trusted individuals can be helpful in ensuring that the person with an eating disorder receives the necessary care and rehabilitation. For some people, treatment may be long term.

Perhaps you have a friend with an eating disorder and you feel you need to help. There is no easy solution. Sometimes any action you take may seem wrong. While it's important for you to be a valuable source of support for your friend, it is also important to encourage them to seek professional help, as eating disorders can have serious medical complications.

On first suspecting that your friend, relative or partner may have this illness, it is important not to alienate the person by reacting too strongly. However, even at this stage it is worth expressing your concern and your willingness to give emotional support. It is important for that person to know there are people who can help.

Whatever you do, don't panic! Look around for the help you need and don't isolate yourself from those who can help or who you may be able to help. Join a support group with your friend or relative. The purpose of a support group is to provide a confidential and safe environment where people can share experiences and draw strength from one another.

If you decide to help your friend deal with their eating disorder, you should try to remain as understanding, open and compassionate as possible. Be informed about the condition by reading as many helpful books and journals as you can on the subject and when you approach your friend, make sure you do it in a confidential and relaxed setting.

Perhaps your friend is in denial and simply cannot or will not accept that she or he has a problem. They may have no motivation to change and they may see the problem as everyone else's and not their own. Try not to be too judgmental, and tell your friend you'll keep supporting them. Keep in touch even if it feels like they are pushing you away.

Perhaps your friend does accept the possibility that they may have a problem, but isn't ready to address it practically. They have accepted the need for change and treatment, but are fearful of taking the next step. You will know when your friend is ready for action because they have made a decision to get help and have an increased need for your support and the support of others. Taking practical action requires strength from both of you, as it often creates emotional turmoil when the reality of the situation hits home.

Once the eating disorder has been dealt with, maintenance of a new healthy lifestyle is the challenge. Change has taken place and now the challenge is relapse-prevention.

Whatever stage your family member or friend may be at, try to avoid confrontation and try not to overreact to whatever they say. Calm, confident strength is vital. Despite approaching the subject carefully, you may need to accept that your friend may not be ready to tackle the eating disorder. Please don't police or try to rescue them, as you will push your friend further away. Let them know they can come to you if they need help. Be present without being intrusive and help your friend to keep perspective when they're trying to win this battle.

It's important that you try not to give too much advice. Be there to listen and encourage your friend to seek professional help but don't try to become a therapist or take responsibility for their problems. You can offer emotional support to your friend but they should also be seeking professional advice.

You may feel as though you simply want to tell your friend to eat more often, but eating disorders aren't just about eating. You need to help your friend take responsibility for themselves. Give them space to express their feelings about eating, but don't tell them what to eat. Avoid getting into major discussions about calories and fat. Instead lead by example, allowing them to see you follow a healthy diet without feeling guilty about what you eat.

If you're very worried about the physical or mental health of your friend, you may feel you need to tell someone. If so, tell your friend what you are going to do and why, and then be prepared for them to feel resentful but know that in the long run, you may be helping them.

prevention

The good news is that there are steps we can take to help prevent the development of an eating disorder:

1.   Examine the ways in which your beliefs, attitudes and behaviors about your own body and the bodies of others have been shaped.

2.   Look closely at your dreams and goals. Do you overemphasize beauty and body shape?

3.   Learn about the dangers of excessive dieting and exercising.

4.   Commit to exercise for enjoyment and energy, rather than to just rid your body of excess fat.

5.   Don't avoid swimming just because you don't like your body shape.

6.   Don't wear clothes that you don't like or that don't fit you properly.

7.   Absorb encouragement and reject criticism about how you look.

freedom

Following are some steps to freedom from turning to food for comfort:

1.   Accept yourself.

2.   Give up perfectionism.

3.   Establish new boundaries.

4.   Don't allow people to walk all over your feelings.

5.   Find alternative means of coping by refocusing.

6.   Reward or comfort yourself in new ways.

7.   Be open to intimate relationships you can trust.

8.   Connect with people from the inside out.

9.   Allow yourself to feel your feelings instead of trying to numb them with food.

10.   Stop thinking about food and start thinking about freedom!

Extreme Behavior

An eating disorder is just one of the many issues that can cause people to make extreme adjustments to their patterns of behavior. Pressure and stressful life circumstances can also lead people to develop addictive or extreme behavior that isn't necessarily food-related. Some addictions may be behavioral, while others may involve a substance, such as drugs or alcohol. People may find themselves addicted to any number of things as they search for a sense of control in the midst of chaotic life circumstances, or seek out a way of escape from a stress-filled reality.

The word "addiction" comes from a Latin term meaning "enslaved by" or "bound to." Addiction is powerful, and actually changes the brain - first by subverting the way it registers pleasure and then by corrupting other normal drives such as learning and motivation.

Experts used to believe that only alcohol and drugs could cause addiction, but more recent research has revealed that certain pleasurable activities, such as gambling, shopping, and sex, can also co-opt the brain.

Behavioral addiction is a type of addiction that involves a compulsion to repeatedly perform a rewarding non-drug-related behavior, regardless of any negative consequences to the person's physical or mental wellbeing. These behaviors may start out as simple coping mechanisms, but can quickly take over a person's life, with devastating consequences. Although breaking an addiction is difficult, it can be done.

Extreme Behavior May Involve:

★   Deliberate self-harm
★   Nail biting or picking
★   Shopping – online or otherwise
★   Online gaming
★   Gambling
★   Over-exercise
★   Sexual activity
★   Food and eating
★   Substance abuse – drugs and alcohol

It isn't always easy to determine whether you have an addiction, or to admit it once you realize it, but acknowledging the problem is the first step toward recovery.

A "yes" answer to any of the following three questions suggests you might have a problem with addiction:

★   Do you use more of the substance or engage in the behavior more often than in the past?
★   Do you have withdrawal symptoms when you don't have the substance or engage in the behavior?
★   Have you ever lied to anyone about your use of the substance or extent of your behavior?

If you think you, or a friend or family member, might be addicted to a substance, activity, object, or behavior, please seek out professional help.

Remember the Truth:
eating disorders and other extreme behavior can be overcome, and healthy balance can be achieved.

balance

You can only find freedom and achieve balance by addressing the following issues that may be holding you back:

1.   **Revelation**
Understand who you are and why you were created.

2.   **Inspiration**
Choose a role model to help inspire you.

3.   **Information**
Know exactly what you have to do.

4.   **Activation**
Decide, then act.

5.   **Motivation**
Find something or someone to help keep you on track.

10 keys to freedom

[from eating disorders and extreme behavior]

Professional help and support are important in dealing with eating disorders and other self-destructive behavior, but all of these keys will help you to deal with the internal and external triggers that can set off an unhealthy relationship with your body. Seek the truth: truth will always lead to FREEDOM.

1. Remember that food is nourishment for your body and should not be used as a weapon.

2. Make a decision to look after your body, but remember, don't become obsessed.

3. Starving yourself will eventually make you fat when you start eating properly again, so don't deprive your body of food.

4. Avoid diet pills and laxatives — they are addictive and can cause long-term health problems.

5. Exercise regularly and eat healthfully.

6. Forgive those who have hurt you. Resentment "eats" away at you on the inside.

7. Don't allow yourself to dwell on the past and on things you cannot change.

8. Don't punish yourself for what is not your fault. Even if it is, solve it and move on. Mature friends and mentors can be a great help with this.

9. Make yourself look in the mirror each day, and even if you don't like what you see yet, tell yourself that you are beautiful because it is the truth.

10. Tell a trusted friend and seek professional help if you feel trapped in any pattern of self-destructive behavior.

body & soul

[action plan]

Body

Respect your body. Learn to deal with stress and anxiety in healthy, life-giving ways. Commit to not starving yourself, commit to eat healthy food, commit to exercise regularly, and you will feel better about yourself.

Soul

Take control of your thoughts and don't allow them to lead you into destructive behavior. The fight for your freedom starts and ends in your heart and mind. Believe that you have what it takes to overcome unhealthy habits. Realign your thinking to ensure you are balanced. Check regularly that your attitude, as well as your body, remains healthy.

My goal is Freedom
FROM EATING DISORDERS & EXTREME BEHAVIOR

my notes

[write your thoughts]

chapter nine

Behind Closed Doors

freedom from abuse
["It takes courage to think forward, and not back."]

sleeping beauty

Once upon a time, a king and queen adopted a little baby girl whom they named Princess Annalise. Princess Annalise was very loved.

All the noblemen and noblewomen of the land were invited to come and bless the baby at her christening except one — the king's brother. He had been banished from the royal court because of his wickedness.

One by one, the noblemen and noblewomen blessed Annalise with a life of virtue and beauty. Then the king's uninvited brother appeared. He stood over the cradle and cursed the baby girl with terrible suffering.

There was a stunned silence. The queen fainted. A kindhearted nobleman came forward and said, "I cannot undo the curse, the child will be hurt, but instead of death she will sleep for a hundred years, until a prince awakens her."

Annalise grew up to be as beautiful and good as the noblemen and noblewomen said she would be. On her fifteenth birthday, the king and queen traveled to the city to buy her gifts. Left alone in the palace, the princess went exploring. She came to an old tower and climbed up the winding staircase. Reaching a large wooden door she pushed it gently and it sprang open.

There stood the king's wicked brother and his two evil sons. The young princess remembered with a shudder the things they had done to her behind closed doors before they were banished. The three men had their wicked way with her and hurt her terribly many times. In terror she fainted and fell to the ground. The evil men left her for dead. The curse of the king's brother had come to pass and Princess Annalise began to shut down, falling into a deep, deep sleep where she was going to heal.

When she was discovered, her parents took her and laid her in a golden bed. In her gown of lace, she looked like a sleeping angel. The kind nobleman who had softened the curse came and touched her forehead with his hand and as he did, the entire palace fell into a deep sleep for a hundred years.

After many years, a prince wandered by the forest and was

intrigued at the sight of the dark palace, partly hidden by huge thorn bushes. He had heard tales of the sleeping princess in a hidden palace. Could the stories be true? When the prince came near the thorn hedge, it parted and let him pass unhurt then closed behind him. Upon entering the palace, he saw the court lying asleep in the great hall. He walked deeper into the castle and came to the tower.

He opened the door and entered the little room where the beautiful princess was sleeping. There she lay, so beautiful that he could not turn his eyes away, and as he stooped down and gave her a kiss, Princess Annalise opened her eyes.

Suddenly, the palace came alive! The whole court awoke and looked at each other in great astonishment. The fire in the kitchen flared and flickered and the maid, who had been motionless, suddenly finished plucking the fowl. A great feast was served and the prince and princess took such joy in each other that they decided to be married. With a wonderful new start and in the process of time, they lived happily ever after.

the end

fact

You may never forget being abused.

truth

Forgiveness is the key that unlocks the freedom to your future.

mirror mirror on the wall ...

why am I the most used and abused of them all?

Bad things do sometimes happen to good people, and that means circumstances beyond our control can end up controlling us. If you have been subject to abuse of any kind, your memory of it can be so vivid it drives you to distraction. You may remember every detail of every single thing that ever happened to you, and it may come to mind daily or even hourly. When this happens, our will is violated and our self-esteem takes a battering.

Oprah Winfrey's childhood was full of pain and suffering from racial issues, comparisons, poverty, her mother and father's separation and being left alone. She was also subjected to horrific sexual abuse from male relatives. At fourteen she became pregnant. The child was born prematurely and died shortly after birth. To cope with the pain and trauma of the abuse she had suffered, she turned to food. She was able to pick herself up and build an amazing public career, but privately, her heart was still in turmoil.

Oprah is anything but a quitter or a loser. Although she hasn't totally won the victory over her weight, she has certainly made bright inroads and she has definitely settled some of the issues that caused her to board the emotional eating roller coaster. That takes courage — to face an issue like abuse head-on. As I said in the introduction, the truth is confronting and it can also be painful.

Courage isn't the absence of fear. Courage is continuing on in the face of fear. Anna Eleanor Roosevelt once said, "You gain strength, courage and confidence by every experience in which you really stop to look fear in the face. You are able to say to yourself, 'I lived through this horror. I can take the next thing that comes along.'" You must do the thing you think you cannot do.

Abuse Defined

Abuse is one of the most significant causes of poor self-esteem and poor body image. There are many types of abuse, including emotional, physical, and sexual.

Emotional (verbal) abuse can include:
★ Teasing
★ Threats
★ Insults
★ Stalking
★ Emotional abandonment (withdrawal)
★ Unreasonable demands
★ Criticizing
★ Belittling
★ Rejection
★ Racism

Physical abuse can include:
★ Hitting
★ Pushing
★ Shoving
★ Burning
★ Shaking
★ Kicking
★ Beatings
★ Tying up
★ Bruising
★ Failing to provide necessities for life

Sexual abuse can include:
★ Forced sexual touching, fondling, kissing or hugging
★ Forced intercourse (vaginal, oral or anal)
★ Forced masturbation on self or abuser
★ Forced incest
★ Forced to watch other people in sexual behavior
★ Rape or involuntary penetration
★ Date rape
★ Forced sodomy
★ Forced exhibitionism and sexual exploitation
★ Forced viewing of pornographic material
★ Forced posing for sexual pictures
★ Sexual torture

Sexual abuse is a serious issue in our society and tragically, it is on the increase, but there is hope for the victims through healing and restoration, and the key is forgiveness. Love and trust also need to find their way back into an impenetrable heart. It may be that you have a broken image of yourself that needs to be restored because abuse of any description can make you feel completely worthless.

Child Abuse

Incest and child sexual assault are sadly becoming more common in our society. Sexual assault happens to girls and boys of all ages, from very young children to teenagers. In most cases the offender is a member of the child's immediate family or someone known and trusted by the child. Though child sexual assault happens to both male and female children, more often the victims are girls. Statistics also indicate that the overwhelming majority of, although not all, offenders are male.

Child sexual assault is basically any sexual behavior imposed on a child. Children are considered to be unable to alter or understand the perpetrator's behavior due to their early stage of development and powerlessness in the situation. The perpetrator's position of authority and trust enables him or her implicitly or directly to coerce the child into sexual compliance, which is why people who have been abused can suffer from a profound sense of powerlessness.

Child sexual assault involves a range of conduct, including:
★   Fondling of the genital area
★   Masturbation
★   Oral sex
★   Vaginal or anal penetration by a finger, penis or any other object
★   Exhibitionism and suggestive behavior or comments
★   Exposure to pornography or age-inappropriate nudity

Any non-accidental physical injury inflicted on a child is considered physical abuse. This may include:
★   Beatings
★   Burns and scalds
★   Fractures

★ Poisoning
★ Bruises or welts
★ Internal injuries
★ Shaking injuries or strangulation

A constant attitude or behavior towards a child that is detrimental to or impairs the child's emotional or physical development is regarded as emotional abuse. This may take the form of:
★ Blame
★ Emotional rejection
★ Isolation
★ Continuing verbal abuse
★ Sexual innuendo

Another form of child abuse is neglect. This is where there is a serious omission or commission by a person that jeopardizes or impairs the child's physical, intellectual or emotional development. A child who is neglected may be:
★ Consistently dirty and unwashed
★ Without appropriate supervision for extended periods of time
★ Undernourished

They therefore may be at risk of:
★ Injury or harm
★ Constant tiredness
★ Hunger
★ Listlessness
★ Medical conditions relating to poor hygiene

A friend of mine was completely neglected as a child and grew up on the streets of Sydney with her brother. Her parents loved her and weren't intentionally cruel, but they were both alcoholics and abusive of each other, and in order to get some peace in their lives, the children fled and lived on the streets. She suffered so much that it is difficult for her to talk about everything that happened; she says she can't remember many things because it was too painful. As a young teenager she developed a goiter, a growth in her thyroid gland, because she was malnourished.

I am delighted to say that my friend is one of the most remarkable women I know. She has a wonderful marriage and lovely children and is now a grandmother. She is using her life to help others get over similar hurdles to those she faced growing up.

Facts About Abuse

The problem of abuse is widespread. Since statistics have been kept by welfare departments, the number of children reported and confirmed as having been abused continues to increase.

This may be due to a number of factors including growing community awareness, professional education, media reports and TV programs, legal requirements and a change in society's attitude towards breaking the silence surrounding family violence.

While a similar percentage of boys and girls were abused by strangers, percentages varied when comparing abuse at the hands of a family member or a known person. 40 percent of boys were assaulted by a family member and 56 percent by a known person, while the percentages for girls is reversed — 56 percent were assaulted by a family member and 40 percent by a known person.

Because an allegation of child sexual abuse provokes such strong emotions, and the consequences to both the family and the alleged offender are so serious, it can sometimes be difficult ensuring that a balanced appraisal is made. That is why it is imperative to seek professional help if you, a friend or a family member has been sexually assaulted.

There is evidence that the immediate effects of severe abuse (physical or sexual) can be catastrophic for children, resulting in mental retardation, brain damage or death. The long-term consequences can also be devastating, leaving physical and emotional scars which result in psychiatric illness, an inability to form meaningful relationships and unusual aggressiveness, which may be turned inward (youth suicide has doubled in the last twenty years) or outward as assault behavior, with the victims repeating the abuse inflicted upon them.

In a study of sexual offenders, it was found that nearly half of them had been child victims of abuse. Not all people who have been abused go on to become abusers, however, many who abuse have been abused themselves. The same pattern is observed in school bullies. Bullies have typically been bullied at some stage, yet not all bully victims go on to become bullies themselves. Parental or self-blame is one catalyst as to why victims sometimes become offenders.

While it is true that severe abuse in childhood can have severe consequences, it is important to acknowledge that an end can be brought to this cycle of abuse. If children feel blamed for their abuse they are more likely to become abusers. However, if the blame is taken from them by a loving adult who instead communicated understanding, protection, and acceptance they are less likely to become abusers themselves.

Generally speaking, evidence suggests that abusive parents have difficulty controlling their impulses, suffer from low self-esteem, a poor capacity for empathy and are socially isolated. Environmental factors such as poverty, poor housing and chronic illness are not sufficient causes, but such stresses combined with poor parenting skills and a sense of having little control over one's life are all contributing factors.

Human Trafficking

Most of us are aware that modern day slavery exists; people are bought and sold and used as goods and services, and this is not acceptable. Human Trafficking is a worldwide problem and it is not tolerable.

The United Nations definition of human trafficking is:
"The recruitment, transportation, transfer, harboring or receipt of persons, by means of the threat or use of force or other forms of coercion, of abduction, of fraud, of deception, of the abuse of power or of a position of vulnerability or of the giving or receiving of payments or benefits to achieve the consent of a person having control over another person, for the purpose of exploitation."

We believe this is our opportunity to do something about this worldwide problem, starting right on our doorstep in our local community.

In the last two years, ICE (Immigration and Customs Enforcement) has discovered approximately one dozen major drop houses throughout Southern California. Human slaves are cheap. In 1850 the average slave cost $40,000 in today's money. Presently a slave costs an average of $90.

Over 50,000 people are trafficked into the U.S. each year as sex slaves, domestics, garment workers and agricultural slaves. And, there are millions of people trafficked within their own countries including the USA, with California being among the top 3 states with the highest concentration of trafficked persons. There are laws here in the U.S. that are in place to protect people from being bought and sold, but this is a 9.5 BILLION DOLLAR industry regardless of the law. This is our opportunity to do something to make a difference, right here, right now.

Domestic Violence

Domestic violence can be defined as a pattern of behavior in any relationship that is used to gain or maintain power and control over an intimate partner. Domestic violence is abuse. Abuse is physical, sexual, emotional, economic or psychological actions or threats of actions that influence another person. This includes any behaviors that frighten, intimidate, terrorize, manipulate, hurt, humiliate, blame, injure or wound someone.

Domestic violence can happen to anyone of any race, age, sexual orientation, religion or gender. It can happen to couples who are married, living together or who are dating. Domestic violence affects people of all socioeconomic backgrounds and education levels.

The statistics are both alarming and tragic:
★   One in every four women will experience domestic violence in her lifetime
★   An estimated 1.3 million women are victims of physical assault by an intimate partner each year
★   85% of domestic violence victims are women
★   Females who are *20-24 years of age* are at the greatest risk of non-fatal intimate partner violence
★   Domestic violence is the leading cause of injury to women
★   Most cases of domestic violence are never reported to the police

Although these statistics are useful, it is widely believed that the incidence of human trafficking and domestic violence is greater than what is currently being reported, as many victims feel unable to speak out. These inaccurate statistics exist because many victims feel unable to speak out. The pressures of negative community attitudes towards them and feelings of shame and fear of retribution from the perpetrator, contribute to low levels of disclosure of violence and other forms of abuse as well.

Also, because domestic violence often occurs in the privacy of the home, there are few outside witnesses. Surveys often require fluency in English, which means that the experience of people from non-English speaking backgrounds may not be adequately represented.

Sleeping Beauty

In my version of the classic fairy-tale *Sleeping Beauty,* what happened to Princess Annalise was one of the most despicable things that can happen to anyone. Sleeping Beauty experienced immeasurable pain as her wicked uncle and his sons sexually abused her. She had come to terms with the fact that she was adopted. She had to deal with the torture of being repeatedly sexually abused. The pain caused the princess to shut down and go to sleep for a very long time.

You may have read this story and realized that this too is your story, and you can relate all too well to the torment, depression and emotional destruction suffered as a result of sexual abuse. If this has happened to you, it's vital for you to realize you did absolutely nothing to deserve what happened to you. It is not your fault. It is not your fault. It is not your fault!

If there was ever going to be a time when someone would want to escape reality, a feeling of wanting to just go to sleep and never wake up again, it would be when they are being abused.

In her book *Breaking Through*, author Cathy Ann Matthews writes about herself, "My history will always read... 'abused as a child.' But now I have found hope. The control of abuse is broken."

Cathy Ann went from sleeping to being able to wake up from the nightmare, because the control of the abuse was broken. She recognized the need to break the power of her past from continuing to rule her future. Cathy Ann used a similar method to the 'Chain of Change' mentioned earlier in this book.

You must face the truth if you have been abused and you need to confront your feelings of self-worth. Seeking help and guidance from someone qualified to help walk you through traumatic memories is something that can allow you to gain the freedom you deserve. Seeking the help you need does not indicate fear or weakness, but rather shows that you value living life the way you were purposed to live. It requires courage for you to make a decision that you will not allow your thinking to revert to your past. This means that every time your thoughts drift backwards, you will need to replace them immediately with thoughts about your future. In time, this will result in positive change and freedom.

Consequences

If you remember being sexually abused, you may have felt or still feel some or all of these feelings:

★   Afraid you've made it up
★   Angry at him or her for what they did
★   Ashamed at not being able to stop it
★   Betrayed by a trusted abuser
★   Scared to tell anyone
★   Anxious and panicked
★   Sad because you lost a part of your child/adulthood life
★   Guilty because you blame yourself
★   Tricked because he or she called it love
★   Angry because no one protected you
★   Depressed
★   Isolated because you couldn't ever tell anyone
★   Insecure and worried about what other people will think
★   Confused about what really happened

The trauma does not end when the abuse stops, and this is common. Sexual abuse can affect a person's life in many ways.

A victim of abuse may hate their body, be unable to trust people, and find intimacy in relationships very difficult; they also may consider sex to be disgusting or humiliating. Then there's the anger. This anger feels the need to destroy. Victims may also "zone out," trying to escape the pain of how they have been affected, physically and emotionally. They may feel like they are going insane and in order to retain some sense of normality, they may even throw themselves into their career so they are busy and on the move all the time — anything to try and escape the pain.

Another common behavior is identified by clinical psychologist John Hodge in Janine Turner's book *Home is Where the Hurt Is*. He says, "It seems that the more desperate the individual is to escape or avoid the memories of what has happened the more and more difficult to deal with and paradoxically more insistent and more persevering they become. Instead of becoming less distressed over time, for some, distress can seem to grow and overwhelm."

Displaced guilt is another consequence in the abuse victim's life. There is a powerful scene in the movie *Good Will Hunting* where Robin Williams is counseling Matt Damon in regard to his delinquent behavior, which was a result of him suffering childhood physical and sexual abuse.

In the movie, Williams tells Damon over and over again that the sexual and physical abuse that he suffered was not his fault. This continues until Damon breaks down and is finally able to acknowledge that it was not his fault. A friend of mine is a counselor and she shows this video to people who have been through abuse, as it helps to illustrate the power of putting the blame where it belongs — off the victim and onto the perpetrator.

It may be that the person who was supposed to be a protector in your life became a perpetrator of pain, and this has led to feelings of shame. This shame can cause you to feel like you have to keep a secret and therefore you may not know how to express yourself because of the crippling fear. Perhaps you have had to learn to go to sleep or shut down on the outside, even though your insides are screaming out with pain and longing to be set free.

A helpful book on this subject is *The Wounded Heart*, by Dr. Dan B. Allender. In this book about hope for adult victims of childhood sexual abuse, Dr. Allender recalls the words of a young woman who was facing memories of abuse perpetrated by her father, "I'd rather be dead than face the truth of the memories."

This is the tragic reality of countless millions of people today — men and women, boys and girls — who are violated and abused and who simply do not know how to deal with their pain. They are too afraid to talk and as a result, they can feel desperately isolated. As they try to solve the problem alone, feeling trapped and unable to escape and with a strong tendency to shut down to deal with the pain, depression can settle like a blanket over their life. Words such as confusion, betrayal, damaged and hopeless are all too familiar to those who have suffered abuse.

Depression

Although depression is not experienced only by those who have been abused, it tends to be more common among those who have. When depressed, life can seem difficult, meaningless, sad and exhausting.

We can go through life feeling like we need to live as everyone expects us to, always cheerful and never tripping over life's problems. There are days when we can feel less than adequate. You are not going "crazy," there is a logical reason for its occurrence and simple steps to dismiss it.

Clinically diagnosed depression is defined as an imbalance of chemicals in the brain and is most commonly brought on as a result of stress. Inside the human brain there are three specific chemicals known as neurotransmitters (serotonin, norepinephrine and dopamine). These three chemicals serve specific functions and it is serotonin that is most often associated with depression.

When the level of serotonin drops in the brain, the result is varying degrees of depression and its corresponding symptoms. At some point in life everyone may experience some form of depression. It may last only a short time, but other cases of depression can last much longer when the serotonin level remains low. We can all probably recount times when we have felt one or more of the following symptoms:

★ Depressed mood
★ Lack of interest in almost all activities
★ Change in appetite
★ Significant weight loss or gain
★ Unusual sleeping behavior
★ Agitation or restlessness
★ Lack of energy or chronic tiredness
★ Low self-esteem or self-depreciation

★   Inability to concentrate or think clearly
★   Desire to escape (run away, lock yourself away)
★   Accelerated thought or worry

It is important to realize that these symptoms can be a natural response by our bodies to disappointing, unexpected tragic events. Experienced only temporarily, they are nothing to be worried about. If you can relate to these symptoms, know you are not alone. Statistics tell us that depression affects one in every ten Americans to some degree.

Unfortunately for many people, the symptoms listed above do not go away and many or even all of these symptoms can be experienced at the same time. In this case it is important to recognize that what you are experiencing is natural, but these behaviors and feelings are not healthy. In fact, they are indicators that things are not normal, and the "emotional pendulum" has swung too far in one direction and needs to be counteracted in order to return the feelings of normality you feel you have lost. There are a number of different causes of depression, including:

★   *Long-term high stress levels*
    This is a type of depression that can sneak up on you. Through daily life, we can have pressures, deadlines, expectations, responsibilities and stresses that go virtually unnoticed. All these seemingly minor things can compound to create a major imbalance of chemicals within the brain. The end result is, "I am depressed but don't know why."

★   *Sudden or severe loss*
    This type of depression is much more easy to recognize. It stems from a radical change, in which the severity of the change leaves the neurotransmitters unable to maintain balance within the brain. It could be caused by abuse, the loss of a friend or loved one, a job loss, or a similar unexpected or severe loss.

Although depression is a psychological condition, it is linked to our physical health. With this in mind, it is important to understand that the way we treat our physical body is going to affect our mental health.

The good news is that depression is almost always treatable and correctable, once properly diagnosed. Through medication the chemical imbalance within the brain can be restored and with the help of a professional psychologist or counselor, the junk and the lies we have filled our minds with can be replaced by the truth. The dark glasses through which you may currently view the world can be removed.

If you are currently taking anti-depressant medication and believe you are now ready to stop taking it, be sure to do so only under the supervision of your trusted medical professional. Going off medication suddenly and without medical supervision can have disastrous consequences.

If you suffer from ongoing depression from what happened in your past, it is time to break the cycle. In *Home is Where The Hurt Is*, author Janine Turner writes, "Everyone has to find their trigger points: those times in their life which remind them of an abusive past." She suggests listing these "triggers" to give you the ability to recognize when you may be most at risk of falling prey to depressive feelings of guilt, shame bitterness, fear and despair.

No More Fear

Having experienced physical and emotional abuse myself, I have known what it is to live in the constant grip of fear. It took me a long time to be able to acknowledge I was not just harmed, but I was abused. I have recollections of bolting out my front door before I could be grabbed and jumping into my car and driving off at a high speed. I used to drive fast on purpose because deep down I wished that the police would pull me over so I could be arrested and rescued. I was never caught. Instead I found myself sleeping on a cold porch at the local Salvation Army shelter. I was too ashamed and afraid to tell anyone what was going on. I loved this person with all of my heart and so I lived with this secret pain for many, many years. I felt worthless and hopeless.

Even though I had been hurt by someone I loved, I needed to get help, and eventually that's exactly what I did. I was then able to draw a boundary line that meant that I wouldn't allow this to happen to me ever again. I became strong enough to draw the line and get out of the abusive cycle. Sadly, many people can't do this and end up in a spiral of depression because they don't know how to stop the pain.

Forgiveness

If you want to deal with the wounds of the past, you will not necessarily feel courageous, nor will you necessarily feel excitement when starting out on a new life journey — the healing process takes time and commitment. You have already lived through the hardest and most painful part — the abuse itself. You have survived and now you can use the strength you have gained to build a future free from the pain of abuse. If you have been abused, you should seek professional help —also:

★ Tell another person that you know you can trust.
★ Forgive those who have hurt you; this will release you from bitterness and reliving the pain.
★ Believe that it wasn't your fault and stop blaming yourself.
★ Feel compassion for yourself, for the person who was frightened and powerless, but don't become self-absorbed.

The only way we can go forward after being subjected to any form of abuse — whether it is sexual, physical or emotional — is to forgive the person or people who have hurt us. However hard it is to do, however painful the experience may have been, if we want to move forward in life, I believe we must forgive.

Forgiveness starts as a decision and then works its way through your life, as you allow it, by giving it room to take over all the pain and bitterness that may be ruling your existence. Genuine forgiveness opens the door again to trust, so that with adequate boundaries (fences, not walls), you will be able to believe again that some people are honest and mean no harm. Some people are safe and reliable, and it is okay to believe them, expect from them and even put hope in them. Forgiveness means we no longer have feelings of anger or resentment towards a person or an action that has caused us harm or distress. We also free someone from their debt towards us. If we don't free them from debt, it will keep that person connected to us for the rest of our lives.

Our forgiveness cuts the cord to the person who has caused us the pain. When we choose to forgive, the past will be the past and not remain in our present or our future.

Remember the Truth:
forgiveness is the key that unlocks
the freedom of your future.

10 keys to freedom
[from abuse]

As you step out from abuse, you will need support from other people. To start with, that may mean a professional counselor and one trusted friend or relative. Expect that these keys will work best when you involve others.

1.   Admit that it happened and do not blame yourself.

2.   Be prepared to face the fact that the abuse has damaged you in some way — your image has been broken.

3.   Work through past pain with a professional counselor.

4.   Recognize how you see yourself, others and relationships.

5.   Explore the habits, attitudes and thought patterns you have developed, and be willing to change them if necessary.

6.   Discover the defense mechanisms you have adopted to stop yourself from being hurt, and adopt positive behaviors to help you deal with any future hurt.

7.   Learn to re-establish appropriate boundaries (see Chapter 6), with the help of others.

8.   Learn to forgive. This is for YOUR benefit and not just for the benefit of the person you are forgiving.

9.   Dare to begin to trust and love.

10.   Reach out and help someone else. Use your past to give someone else hope for the future.

body & soul
[action plan]

Body

Allow people you trust to touch you. Allowing hugs from people you trust will help you get over some of the fears associated with being physically violated.

Soul

Change the track in the playback device of your mind. Don't listen to past abusive words, and do listen to, believe in and live out becoming the wonderful person you really are. Believe for healing and the ability to forgive those who have hurt you, and believe that your story will one day be able to help others.

**My goal is Freedom
FROM ABUSE**

my notes

[write your thoughts]

chapter ten

Stand Tall Princess

freedom from envy and jealousy
[We should celebrate achievement,
innovation and creativity in our own lives
and in the lives of others.]

Snow White

Once upon a time, a beautiful royal couple lived in a magnificent palace. One winter day, as the queen sewed beside her window, she accidentally pricked her finger. As she stared at the drops of blood falling on the snow outside her window, she thought of her daughter, with skin as white as snow, lips as red as blood and hair as black as ebony. The queen called her Snow White.

Snow White was very close to her mother and when she died suddenly, Snow White was crushed with grief. But time passed and the king married again. The woman he married was attractive, but she was very cold and very jealous of Snow White. The new queen spent hours staring at her mirror, asking,

"Mirror, mirror on the wall, who's the fairest of them all?" The mirror was magical, and it answered her, "You are the fairest of them all."

But Snow White was growing up and becoming lovelier. She was beautiful, strong and smart.

One day the queen approached her mirror, and it said, "Listen, Queen, what I tell you is true, Snow White is far lovelier than you!" The Queen was enraged and she forced a servant to leave Snow White deep in the forest at the mercy of wild beasts.

Snow White wandered alone until she came to a tiny cottage. Exhausted, she curled up on one of the seven little beds and fell asleep. When the seven dwarves who lived there arrived home, Snow White awoke and explained how she had come to the forest and all that had happened to her in the palace. The friendly little dwarves encouraged Snow White to stand tall.

The kind men invited her to stay, and the next day they warned Snow White to be very careful of the Queen, because the mirror would surely tell her the truth about her whereabouts: "You, O Queen, are the fairest here, but over the hills, in the greenwood shade, where seven dwarves their house have made, there Snow White is hiding from you, and she is far lovelier than you!"

The queen decided to take matters into her own hands. Disguised as an old woman, she walked to the cottage and knocked on the door. Snow White looked up to see an old lady selling apples. "Try one," she said. Snow White took a bite from the poisoned apple and immediately collapsed.

"Nothing will save you now!" cried the queen triumphantly. As the queen ran back into the darkness, it overtook her. She fell down in utter surprise, depression and anguish, not feeling one bit as victorious and free as she thought she would. "I got rid of her," she thought. "I should feel free! Why do I feel worse?" The darkness crowded in around her. "I refuse to help her! I will not love her!" she screamed into the night. But no one heard her, no one saw her and no one has seen or heard from her since.

When the seven dwarves returned home they found their beautiful friend without breath. Laying her on a bed, they wept for days. They wanted somewhere special for Snow White to rest.

A handsome prince visited the dwarves as they mourned and offered to take the beautiful girl to his palace, where she could lie. As the Prince lifted her limp body, a small piece of apple fell from her mouth, and she awoke. "Where am I?" she whispered.

"You are safe," said the prince gently. The Prince took Snow White to his palace, where they fell deeply in love. Snow White stood with her head held high with the handsome Prince by her side. They returned to the palace where she was reunited with her father and they all lived and reigned in the kingdom, happily ever after.

the end

Fact

Jealousy is an ugly shade of green.

truth

A blessed life is admirable.

mirror mirror on the wall ...

who's the fairest of them all?

Many people define success in terms of how satisfied they are with their personal and professional relationships. In fact, a great deal of our overall happiness in life can be influenced by achieving success in these personal and professional realms. However, our desire for success can sometimes lead to the harmful emotions of jealousy and envy. Many people who are beautiful, smart and talented are made to feel guilty for it because beauty and brilliance can cause jealousy in others.

The more we shine, the more some people tend to feel threatened and there can be a cruel pressure in life to shrink rather than stand tall. It is crucial to recognize when people are trying to cut you down to size so that you don't automatically shrink in their presence. Resist the pressure and learn to stand tall and shine, just as you were created to shine. When you maintain a deep sense of knowing that you have been created for a purpose greater than yourself, you simply won't allow yourself to be kept in a box.

On the other hand, you might find yourself falling into the pattern of cutting others down to size, or wanting what they have for your own life. The more you focus on your own gifts and goals, the less you will yearn for what someone else has. This chapter deals with both aspects of jealousy and envy, whether you are receiving it or sending it out.

Jealousy

Most of us have experienced the "green-eyed monster," jealousy, as described in Shakespeare's famous play *Othello*. At its highest intensity it is a horrible, tormenting obsession and often involves power and control, as we want to keep things or people exclusively to ourselves. Yet just as falling in love seems natural and uncontrollable, so too can jealousy. It just comes over us when someone or something threatens what we have.

In order to work out how we should behave to maintain healthy self-esteem for ourselves and others, it's important to understand that jealousy is not always negative. Like hunger and thirst, feelings of jealousy (and envy) are normal symptoms of one or more unfulfilled human needs. Accepting this can help you be free from unwarranted guilt or shame.

One of the first things we need to understand about jealousy is that it is a word used to describe a variety of emotional states that are not all the same. It is confusing when, for example, the same word is used to describe the pain we might feel at learning our partner has been unfaithful, and the suspiciousness of a person who is constantly seeing signs of infidelity where none in fact exists. One form of jealousy is rational and the other form is irrational.

Unhealthy jealousy and irrational behavior usually go hand in hand. Sometimes this behavior results in the destruction of people and possessions, all in the name of not wanting to lose something; as the saying goes, "If I can't have it, then no one will," or "If I can't be with them, then no one will." So we systematically destroy that which we are so desperate to preserve. All because we aren't secure enough to set people free.

Jealousy that comes from being protective of your relationships is rational, as long as you give the people and relationships in your life freedom to have a life outside you. I personally like the fact that my husband is jealous in a healthy way of our marriage and family; that is, if anyone were to try to interfere with it in a negative way, he would fight to protect it. This kind of concern brings security.

As the famous saying goes, "If you love someone, set them free. If they come back, they're yours. If they don't, they never were." If you want to safeguard your relationships by having healthy self-esteem, then you need to gain security and lose unhealthy jealousy that will only make the person whose relationship you value want to run far away from you.

Jealousy is a very primitive emotion that is displayed at a very young age in each one of us. It is simply the emotion of possessiveness. Young children often display it when they say "That's mine!" before grabbing something back.

There are two basic sources of jealous feelings. The first is internal and is based upon low self-esteem, a sense of inferiority or preoccupation with loss. The second is external and occurs in response to an actual or perceived loss of attention or caring from someone. Usually there is a blend of both internal and external factors that work together in a self-perpetuating cycle.

Most instances of jealousy arise from insecurity, but sometimes jealousy comes from feelings of scarcity rather than feelings of insecurity in oneself — the fear is that "there is only so much love to go around."

Those who suffer from jealousy are usually vigilant and anxiously watchful. They are also apprehensive about the motives of others and they usually have a morbid fear of rivalry in love, career or assets.

Suspicion is also an aspect of jealousy. We are jealous when we suspect someone of aiming to deprive us of what we dearly prize. Basically, the greater the threat, the more intense the jealousy. How we perceive the threat influences the jealousy.

Five Stages of Jealousy

The following five stages of jealousy reflect what this cycle of emotion can look like:

1. Suspicion
If you are insecure about a situation and you are very dependent on another person, you may be jealous. You may see signs of problems when none are there.

2. Assessment
We may over focus on certain situations and lie awake at night worrying and reviewing any evidence we may have. When it comes to relationships, men often see a threat and feel jealous first, then worry something is wrong with them, whereas women are more concerned with maintaining the relationship. They worry about losing love; they feel inadequate first, then jealous.

3. Emotions
If we decide there is a threat to something we have, we can have a very wide range of responses: clinging dependency, violent rage at the competitor or the partner, fear, obsessive curiosity, self-criticism, depression, suicidal thoughts, hurt, resentment and

244   Mirror Mirror by Dianne Wilson

social embarrassment.

4. Coping

There are two basic choices. The first is to try and do whatever it takes to secure that which is threatened, and the other is to try and protect your feelings when everything's over. The preservation of self-respect is important when it comes to getting on with the future after losing something or someone has been taken from you.

5. End Result

It is important to know whether particular emotional and coping responses are going to help or harm you. Ask yourself whether these responses will build or destroy what is left of your self-esteem.

Jealousy, and also envy, may have different meanings and emotional associations for different people, depending on the cultural influences they grew up with. Being jealous or envious may feel acceptable to some people as a normal, usually harmless human trait, while with others, jealousy may cause them to feel that they are experiencing something wrong.

When our self-esteem is low and when we are unaware of what we are feeling or thinking, we tend to handle negative emotions by becoming uncomfortable in the situation, by blaming someone else; then we react with negative emotions which cause us to feel worse, and so we increase the blame.

Getting beyond the negative emotions that come with the unhealthy jealousy and envy package, we need to stop blaming everyone else and start taking responsibility for why we are feeling what we are feeling and how we are reacting. Otherwise, we will find ourselves stuck in the blame merry-go-round, which is an unhealthy cycle that says, "I am a poor victim."

The way to deal with this cycle is to assess why you are feeling jealous or envious and then when it comes time to allocate responsibility, recognize right then that you have a part to play in controlling how you are going to react. Once you take control, you are able to dissipate your emotions.

Envy

We sometimes use the terms jealousy and envy interchangeably, but they are two different words with two different meanings. Despite the frequent confusion of these two terms, a clear distinction remains. Envy is defined as "a feeling of discontent and resentment aroused by and in conjunction with desire for the possessions or qualities of another," while jealousy is being 'fearful or wary of being supplanted, apprehensive of losing affection or position.'

If I want what you have, I am envious of you. If, however, I want to protect something I have from you, I am jealous of that particular thing.

Deep down, people who are unhealthily jealous do not necessarily want to be rich so much as they want others to be poor. Envy sees that you are rich and wants the same for itself. Here is a clear distinction between jealousy and envy: envy desires the value, but jealousy desires to destroy that value in someone else's life. The jealous reaction to someone or something of value is usually not love, desire and admiration, but the opposite — hate, rejection and disdain.

Unhealthily jealous people usually try to hide their mission to destroy the valuable behind noble causes, or talk about wanting to bring people down to size. Unhealthy envy comes from recognizing values and virtues but failing to achieve them personally. These types of people often resent success, happiness, achievement and any good fortune. They rejoice in others' failures.

Because jealousy is more about "me" and envy more about "you," the former is often displayed in a much more active and sometimes violent manner than the latter. Don't get caught believing that either you or someone else is jealous or envious only if displaying more aggressive emotions, such as anger. One can feel anxiety as opposed to anger, and still be envious or jealous.

Just as with some jealousy, not all feelings of envy need to be seen as negative. For example, it is certainly not wrong to look at a healthy marriage and want a healthy and happy marriage for yourself. We can often look enviously at people who are very blessed in body and soul, and wish we could have what they have. They have an enviable life, which means that people are drawn to want the same blessing, and as long as it's for the right reasons, then there is nothing wrong with this type of desire. If you have special feelings of animosity directed toward that person, however, then you are negatively envious of them.

When you experience either jealousy or envy, it doesn't make you a bad person. Learning how to handle them is extremely important for our emotional wellbeing and self-esteem. The main concern is not so much whether we experience jealousy or envy, but what we should do when we have these experiences. If you choose to explore why you feel the way you do, then you have an opportunity to get to the bottom of the emotion. When you understand why you feel jealous or envious, then you can begin to deal with it.

I don't think anyone is immune from either jealousy or envy. As I've said, I don't think people are necessarily wrong to have these feelings, or that they should be suppressed. After all, suppression of anything, and especially emotions, does not make them disappear. And I am most definitely not saying I have never experienced envy or jealousy.

However, the occasions have become less and less as I have grown to accept that my focus should be within my own life.

When I do feel those twinges of emotion, I view them as signals telling me something. Either my focus is not in the right place, or I have an insecurity or fear which has nothing to do with the other person, and must be dealt with.

Both envy and jealousy, in my opinion, mean self-focus. This is the beginning of the end when it comes to developing healthy self-esteem. While we must take care of ourselves, we should not be the center of the universe to ourselves. This is selfish and unhealthy living.

Take your eyes off what you don't have, or what others have, and turn the scanner within. Find the cause of your envy and jealousy, clear away past negative voices and experiences, then pour some energy into building your personal and emotional security. Then you will be the one others envy, and you can remember the pain and reach out to them.

When unhealthy envy and jealousy are present in your life, they bring discontentment and resentment because of one person's yearning for something possessed by another. This something can be physical or invisible. The longing, and the related relationship stresses, are just the same, and some jealousies are worse than others. Like all relationship problems, unhealthy envy and jealousy can be seen as either a problem or an opportunity. You have a choice to live with resentment, hurt, anxiety and guilt, or with encouragement, empathy, compassion and constructive internal growth.

Needless to say, the best protection against envy and jealousy is a healthy self-esteem; that is, prevention is better than cure. Envy and jealousy can be reduced by staying active, distracting yourself with friends, being involved in fun activities, furthering your career, undertaking steps for self-improvement where necessary, and renewing your mind. Before long, the many irrational thoughts and expectations that come with envy and jealousy will be defeated with rational thinking.

Snow White

In the classic story *Snow White*, a young woman was hunted down by someone who was insanely jealous of her beauty. Most people at some time during their lives have either been subjected to, or taken part in, jealous or envious behavior or both. It is human nature, and jealousy is not just confined to romance. Romantic or relational jealousy is obvious, but other types of jealousy are more subtle and yet can be equally or more destructive.

Snow White became victim to another's jealousy and envy. She was obsessively envied, harassed and hunted down — all because she was fairer than them all. The sad reality is that some people live their lives at a level below their full potential, even though they may be beautiful and bright, simply because they have been subjected to another person's jealousy of them and they have not known how to deal with it. This can cause some people to wish they were just like everyone else, not standing out in any way at all.

The wicked queen didn't just want to bring Snow White down to size, but down to a size that was smaller than herself, so she could feel better about who she was.

Despite their size, the seven dwarves were the exact opposite. They nurtured and encouraged Snow White so she grew even taller.

They may have been small in physical stature, but by seeing who Snow White really was and not being intimidated by a princess and the "greatness" that she had within her, they encouraged her to fulfill that greatness, and were therefore giants on the inside.

Envy vs Admiration

When you have a healthy self-esteem, your strongest response to seeing someone else succeed in any area will be admiration rather than jealousy or envy. You will want to congratulate them and cheer them on, or perhaps even find out how they got to be successful in that area, rather than desiring to see their success taken away from them.

Be happy for someone else's success, and one day you too may enjoy similar success. The best protection against jealousy is a healthy self-esteem. Prevention is better than cure!

Gifts and Talents

We all have gifts and the potential for talent in something. You might not see yours in your "mirror" because of others' jealousy or envy, or because of your lack of, or excess, self-esteem. But they are there.

Gifts are the abilities we "just have" and are often called natural abilities. Giftedness means that you have and use untrained and instinctive abilities in at least one field of endeavor. Talent refers to your ability to master steadily developed abilities (or skills) and knowledge in at least one field of human activity at a superior level.

According to Professor Francois Gagne, who developed a model of giftedness and talent, the outcome of these abilities should place you in the top 15 percent of your age group if they are to be classed as being a gift or talent. He also states that gifts can progress to talent through systematic learning and training, but not talent to gifts — gifts are the foundation for talent.

Gifts and talents can be progressed or hindered by two types of factors: intrapersonal and environment. Intra-personally, motivation plays the most crucial role in initiating any move to further develop talent — it guides it and sustains the gift through things such as failure. What is great is that motivation can be developed in us — so we all have the opportunity to grow our gift by increasing our motivation, and not simply leaving it to genetic disposition. Environmentally, influences can be microscopic or macroscopic. Microscopic environmental influences include upbringing and socioeconomic status and macroscopic influences include your geography (where you live) and demography (who else lives there). Again, these things can be changed and therefore your gift increased to talent.

What is also important to note is those things that will hinder your talent development. Peer pressure, the death of a family member or close friend, or being involved in a major accident or incident can not only hinder self-esteem, but may also keep your talent from finding expression so it remains locked inside you. If you can increase your self-esteem, you increase your chances of unlocking your talent. You'll also find that if you start to work on your talent, and gain mastery in an area, this will help increase your sense of self-esteem.

Gifts and talents help give us drive and motivation in life — they should therefore be a source of great enjoyment to us. And it is often the recognition of this by others that results in feelings of jealousy and envy, so they choose to attack that area in your life and try to steal it from you. Don't let it happen! You need to see yourself as valuable and valued. The truth is, there is no one else on earth like you, gifted exactly as you are. You are not dispensable, if you don't want to be you — there will be no other that could be. Take your gifts and talents seriously, find out what they are. Poor self-esteem can distort your perception of what your gift or talent is, as can an unhealthy enlarging of it.

Sometimes we just won't allow ourselves to see our true gifts and talents because of mind-sets that tell us the gift and talent we have is not good enough. This mind-set can come from many areas, often from being rejected before in that area. But don't give up. Gifts and talents can help us realize our dream, so don't let someone stomp on it because it isn't what they have, or because they can't have it or don't want you to have it.

And don't forget about valuable family and friends. Good family and friends can sometimes spot things we miss and, if you ask them what they think you may be gifted or talented at, it can help you pinpoint it a little more.

Once you have identified a gift or talent, or have a hunch about one, get involved and use the talent. If you think it may be music then buy music and an instrument (or borrow or rent one), take lessons, watch video tutorials about it, find someone you look up to with that same gift or talent and hang out with them — find out what they do to improve their gift or enjoy it, join a band, organize 'jam sessions' for you and your friends, or just play by yourself if this seems a little too difficult for you to start off with.

The idea is to get involved in that area of gifting or talent and equip yourself in it. You have to feed something in order for it to grow, so feed your gift and talent. It will have this wonderful cyclic effect of improving your self-esteem, which will increase your confidence, which will in turn increase your gift or talent, which in turn again will increase your self-esteem.

Exercising your gifts and talents creates win–win situations.

So how do you recognize if you are gifted or talented in something? First, you need to ask yourself what it is that you feel may be your gift or talent.

gifted & talented

If you can strongly agree with the majority of the statements below, it is more than likely that the skill or activity you are wondering about is a gift or a talent in you.

1.   I learn easily and quickly in this area.

2.   After little or no training I have success in this area.

3.   It is a passion of mine.

4.   I get great results in this area.

5.   I recognize it as a talent and ability, in myself.

6.   Other people comment on my ability in this area.

7.   I really enjoy doing this and don't get easily bored.

Don't panic if you can't respond to one of the above statements — your self-esteem may be quite low, but as you build this up (by following the advice set out for you in the previous chapters), you will be amazed at what you can do!

Establishing Your Call

Nature is an amazing thing. Have you ever taken the time to sit among it all and just observe? It is great for the body and the soul. What has amazed me over and over again as I observe nature is the way everything moves and connects together. One of those connections is in the way different animals communicate to each other. How does a lamb know its mother from the hundreds of other ewes in the field? The mother has a specific call, just for her baby. How does the male seal find his partner among the hundreds of identical females that are scattered across the shore? A call. It is meant for only one, and only that one can really answer the call. If another lamb tried to approach the mother ewe, she would reject it — as the bull seal would reject another female.

You and I have a "call." It is what you were destined to do and only you can answer or fulfill it — as it is meant only and specifically for you. Of course, just because you have a call doesn't mean you will answer or fulfill it and just like our gifts and talents, the jealousy and envy we feel or that others subject us to can hinder or even prevent our call from being realized.

I know what it is like to be envied in an unhealthy way, and I don't like it. I know what it is to have someone want to try and steal my identity. But try as they may, they can't take away who I am, no matter how manipulative and envious they become. This is an example of unhealthy and damaging jealousy and envy, and when an individual tries to do this, it is a sign that their self-esteem is extremely low — otherwise they wouldn't be trying to be someone they are not.

Regardless of whether you suffer from unhealthy jealousy or envy or both, you need to take charge of your feelings and emotions by thinking about and taking responsibility for your actions. One way of doing this is by looking at your own life and focusing on everything that you are and what you are meant to be doing with your life. As you learn to focus on your own "lane" in life, you become less concerned with feeling the need to have someone else's life.

Following is an example of how to take a good look at what you are meant to be doing with your life.

I have dissected my call as follows:

Me

I am called to be me. That's an important revelation I must have before I can even begin to focus on what I am meant to be doing with my life. I am also called to ensure I am healthy in body and soul. This means I need to eat well, exercise regularly and get enough sleep! I also need to feed my soul by taking time out for recreational activities. I feed my spirit by reading books filled with light, life and love, and by being part of a community of people with similar values and beliefs. Looking after 'me' means I can focus on all the other things I am meant to do with my life.

Mission

Ever since I was a little girl I have wanted to help people. I know that part of my call is to help make a positive difference in people's lives. I have chosen to do this through writing and speaking, helping people in the areas of body and soul. In my younger years I thought the only way of achieving this desire in my heart was to choose one or the other, but I have since learned that many people need help in all three areas, and they are so closely linked it now makes sense for me to focus on helping people holistically.

Marriage

I am very much in love with my husband and am very happily married. As I mentioned in Chapter 1, my first marriage ended sadly in divorce. Just because it didn't work out the first time, did not mean I wasn't called to be married. I believe that marriage is meant to be part of my life, and therefore it forms part of my call. A healthy marriage requires both partners to contribute in a positive and nurturing way, and it requires commitment, selflessness and much unconditional love. With all those vital ingredients (and more), this is a call that is one of the most wonderful things two people in love can do together.

Motherhood

I always dreamed of someday becoming a mommy and now I can honestly say that all of my dreams (and more) have come true. I am head over heels in love with all my babies and I consider my call to motherhood one of the most important roles in my life. And my children help me keep perspective about what is really important! At the end of my life the most important things to me will be my family, and what I have been able to invest into their lives.

Marketplace

Most of us need to work. If we don't we'll starve! I believe our vocational call is incredibly important. We spend most of our lives and waking hours at work, so it's vitally important not to spend all of that time wasting your life away, doing something that you utterly despise. If you look at your vocation as a call, it places a different emphasis on it. If what is important to you is job satisfaction, then perhaps taking a pay-cut in order to have that satisfaction fulfilled is what you need to do. However, if working to make money is what you believe you are called to do, then focus on the rewards at the end of the day. Whatever way you decide to look at your vocational call, you should take the time to ask yourself, 'Is this what I'm really meant to be doing with my life?'

When you live out your calling, you move into a fantastic league called the Super Achievers.

Super Achievers

In his book *Secrets of Super Achievers*, Philip Baker writes in praise of tall poppies and the abundance mentality that they should all have.

He says that although there are many people on the ladder of success who believe that in order to get to the top they have to dislodge or remove those above them and walk all over those beneath them, some do not. Success isn't a ladder as much as a journey on a road that has enough room for everyone. The travelers on this road are better off helping those with them than attacking them.

Jealousy doesn't reflect that you have what it takes to be a super achiever; it only reflects your intense needs, your desperation to keep what you want, and unrealistic demands about what the future may hold for you. It wants to say, "I win, you lose." Therefore jealousy reflects self-interest and self-love, rather than mutual reciprocal love that not only sets you free, but other people too. Super achievers do not operate with an "I win, you lose" mentality, but with an "I win, you win," attitude to life.

This may surprise you, as stereotypically we envisage super achievers to be ruthless and aggressive — disregarding the cost. When you study the lives of those who qualify as super achievers, this type of attitude is rare.

Super achievers understand that individual success does not necessarily mean the failure of others. They have, what Baker terms, an "abundance mentality." They want to succeed, they want to do well, they want to reach their goals and they are not in any way hampered by a feeling of guilt. Guilt only accompanies those who think in terms of "I win, you lose."

A genuine super achiever is never threatened by someone else's success. They don't allow jealousy or envy to dominate their thinking processes. We must realize that our own success should help others and not hinder them. When this is understood, we will move out of the fog of self-interest and the destructive style of confrontational competition, into the clear light of freedom and achievement.

Don't get trapped in small-minded, jealous and envious thinking. Life is like an ocean. There is plenty of water for everyone.

Why be jealous or envious of someone when you can still achieve your goal in the future? It is only you who will stop and block what you rightfully deserve. Take some time to dissolve the jealousy and move on. If you saw something you liked but were unable to achieve it, then learn from the last experience so that next time it comes along you will be able to achieve it. Previously, it might not have been the right time or it was better that the other person receive the reward; it doesn't matter. Accept and don't dwell on it, move on and concentrate on the next goal and how you will be able to achieve it — and not how you missed out.

If you allow yourself to open your mind and see what you were called to achieve, you can have true love, a good job, and everything positive that your heart desires. You just need to trust and believe in yourself to allow what you deserve to come into your life. Do not limit yourself and try to understand the unseen process of life. There are many factors that you will not see, but you just have to accept that it might not have been the right time. When you are ready, it will come to you easier than expected because the natural flow of life allows right experiences to come to the right people at the right time.

You can spend as much time as you want thinking about things you have missed out on, but it will not change the event that caused the jealousy in the first place. Being jealous will not help, but will hinder you in the future. Alexandre Dumas once said, "Jealousy is the art of injuring ourselves more than others." Your thoughts should be put into more positive areas by learning from that experience so you too can achieve more in the future.

You must learn to accept and move on and not dwell on the past; recognize that it is the past and you are now in a different time and place, so it is not worth holding on to.

If you find yourself having a jealous thought, make a strong effort to stop. Admit to yourself that this is a jealous thought and that you can control what you think. Remind yourself that you are just as good as the person you are feeling jealous of. Don't allow yourself to go down the jealous thought road. Cut the negative, unhealthy jealous thoughts off and concentrate on your own strengths instead. Stand tall, princess. Your shrinking and jealousy of others serves no purpose. You are meant to be tall on the inside. Your shrinking will only prevent you from achieving your potential and keep you living a sub-standard existence.

Quit shrinking!

**Remember the Truth:
a blessed life is admirable.**

stand tall

Our deepest fear is not that we are inadequate.
Our deepest fear is that we are powerful beyond measure.
It is our light, not our darkness, that most frightens us.
We ask ourselves, "Who am I to be brilliant?"
Actually, who are you not to be?
Your playing small doesn't serve the world.
There's nothing enlightened about shrinking so that other people won't feel insecure around you.
And as we let our own light shine, we unconsciously give other people permission to do the same.
As we are liberated from our own fear, our presence automatically liberates others.

Marianne Williamson
"A Return to Love"

you can...

"What I do you cannot do; but what you do,
I cannot do.
The needs are great, and none of us,
including me, ever do great things.
But we can all do small things, with great love,
and together we can do something wonderful."

Mother Teresa of Calcutta

10 keys to freedom

[from jealousy]

Some of these keys relate to being jealous or envious of others, while some refer to being the subject of jealousy or envy. Apply what seems most important in your particular situation.

1.   Stand tall.

2.   Don't deny who you really are and put yourself in positions where you require yourself to be something or someone you are not.

3.   Bless, or at least ignore, those who curse you, and they will eventually go away.

4.   Don't despise your beauty.

5.   Grow in wisdom and understanding.

6.   Nurture your virtue.

7.   Never pull anyone down to size — that's not your job in life.

8.   Cut any negative, unhealthily jealous thoughts off.

9.   Recognize that your were born on purpose for a purpose.

10.   Keep dreaming a bigger dream for your life.

body & soul

[action plan]

Body

Don't shrink in situations where you feel less than someone else or where you feel like you are standing out too much. Watch your posture. Be you and stand tall, from the inside out.

Soul

Desire and work towards attaining the positive qualities you see in others without crossing the line and becoming jealous of them, or obsessed about your own shortfalls. Believe that you can become a person who deflects jealousy, and whose life is one to be positively envied, for all the right reasons.

**My goal is Freedom
FROM JEALOUSY**

my notes

[write your thoughts]

chapter eleven

Pit to Prison to Palace

freedom from discouragement
["The test of confinement is when people try to box you
into something that your dream wants to set you free from."]

joseph the dreamer

Once upon a time, there was a young boy named Joseph. He was a dreamer and each of his dreams reflected his future, like a mirror. Now, Joseph had ten older brothers who hated him. Of all the boys, Joseph was the favorite son of Jacob, their father. He made Joseph a magnificent coat of many colors and because of it, his brothers despised him even more.

One day Joseph explained to his brothers a dream he'd had that showed him in a position of favor above them. This made their hatred towards him grow stronger. They stripped him of his beautiful coat and threw him into a pit, then sold him to some passing traders. They returned home to their father without him. Thinking that some wild animals had killed Joseph, Jacob wept over the loss of his favorite son.

Joseph was taken to Egypt as a slave where his new owner, Potiphar, favored Joseph and grew to trust him — putting him in charge of his household. Potiphar's wife was very pleased because she was infatuated with Joseph. She tried to seduce him but Joseph resisted, refusing to put his future on the line.

Offended by Joseph's refusal, Potiphar's wife sought revenge — she lied to her husband, saying that Joseph had tried to seduce her! Potiphar was extremely upset at Joseph's alleged betrayal of him and had him thrown in prison. There, Joseph met two of the king's servants — a butler and a baker. One night these two men each had dreams that they could not understand and they told Joseph, who interpreted them. The dreams showed that the butler would be released but that the baker would die.

Shortly after, the king reinstated the chief butler but he hanged the chief baker, just as Joseph had predicted. Instead of thanking Joseph, the chief butler forgot him and so Joseph remained in prison. Years passed and the king himself had dreams that no one could interpret. He was troubled and wanted to know their meaning. Finally, the chief butler remembered Joseph, who was still in prison. Immediately the king summoned Joseph, who said that his dreams predicted seven years of plenty in the land followed by seven years of famine. He said it would be wise for someone to manage a great storehouse in preparation for the years of lack. The king was pleased and he appointed Joseph to manage the storehouse.

When the great famine struck, Jacob sent his sons to buy grain from the King of Egypt. They came before their brother Joseph, but they did not recognize him. Joseph gave his brothers grain and asked about their family. They did not understand his questioning, but they answered meekly because of Joseph's position of authority.

When the grain in Jacob's household ran out, the brothers returned once again to Joseph's storehouse. This time, Joseph revealed his identity. They were very afraid because of what they had done to him, but Joseph was not angry or vengeful. He was full of love and forgiveness. He saw that every turn in his life, good and bad, had been used to build the person he had eventually become.

The brothers went home and brought their father and their families to the prosperous land where their brother Joseph now lived. Jacob was overjoyed that his son was alive and they all lived happily ever after.

the end

fact

Life is a series of expansions and contractions.

truth

Within every contraction lies the seed of an expansion.

mirror mirror on the wall ...

why don't my dreams come true at all?

One of the most powerful parts of a human being is the mind. It's the directional part of our being which dictates what we believe about ourselves and why. Our heart may be where dreams begin, but our mind is where dreams are formulated and facilitated.

Dreams are not limited to our sleeping hours. Dreams are also our hopes and desires for our lives. Everyone has dreams and goals, even if they are hidden. Dreams live in a place deep within, bringing you comfort in times of pain, where you can picture how you would like your life to be, the places you want to go, the person you wish to be, the things that you want out of life and what you would like to achieve.

Dreams don't just come true without effort and passion. See if you can relate to some of the following patterns of a dreamer.

A dreamer dreams that their ordinary life will become extraordinary. They dream that their past and present situation will bow down to their future. They dream that their dream will see the light of day and that it will actually come true. They dream that their dream will make a difference to their life and to the world.

A dreamer dreams that they will enjoy a fulfilled and prosperous existence with a healthy body and soul; they dream of making other people's dreams live. They dream that their dream will live on after they die and that it will become a legacy to the next generation. Part of the journey to seeing our dreams fulfilled is dealing with self- doubt, disappointment and discouragement. All of us, at some point in time, have to deal with these things. Discouragement is universal; no one is exempt from it. From the richest to the poorest, all have to deal with times of discouragement. I know that all of us would like to think we are immune to discouragement, but the truth is we're not.

We all experience times of insecurity and uncertainty as to our future and our place in this world. But know that you have a secret treasure chest within, the place you hold dear to your heart, that only you know. This is the place where you hold your innermost dreams and desires. These dreams and desires are still there, even if you have spent years trying to ignore and suppress them, pretending they are not there.

Discouragement

Discouragement is losing the desire and motivation to continue doing something that brings purpose and satisfaction to one's life. To discourage is to dampen or destroy the courage, depress the spirit or lessen self-confidence, to dishearten or deter. We start doing something new, filled with excitement and enthusiasm, and partway through discouragement tends to visit. It is up to us whether we allow it to set in or not.

Discouragement can be contagious. If you are around someone who is deeply discouraged, then they can discourage you if you are not prepared to deal with it. We cannot isolate ourselves from those who are discouraged, but we can protect ourselves by focusing on our dreams. Contagious does not mean 'incurable.'

While we may get discouraged from time to time, we must never allow discouragement to become part of our identity. We don't have to stay locked into a lifestyle of discouragement. There is a difference between experiencing discouragement and living discouraged.

Sometimes we can look at what we are doing and it may look like we are making little or no progress at all. It may seem the more we work, the less we accomplish. Yet we must never allow ourselves to believe we are beyond hope. People may feel discouragement for a number of reasons.

Fatigue
This may be physical, mental or emotional. Fatigue and discouragement often hit halfway through a project. We tend to start with loads of energy, but after a while the freshness of a new project tends to wear off and boredom, weariness and discouragement can set in. That's why so many people fail to complete what they start.

After working hard and long, it can seem that our accomplishments don't match the energy or the effort we have put in. When we are tired, we tend to see things differently from how they really are. Tiredness blurs our vision and dulls our dreams.

Frustration

The word frustrate means to break, to annul, to do away with, to fail, to render ineffective, to split, to divide. We become frustrated when we lose sight of our purpose and goals in life. Frustration sets in when you never quite finish a task. We can all overcome and be effective in what we do, but if we allow ourselves to be overcome by frustration and discouragement we will fail to realize our dream.

Doubt

Doubt is a loss of confidence in something or someone and is a major contributor to discouragement. If we find ourselves doubting our vision, we lose the ability to see how to live a productive life. When we lose our confidence we lose heart. When we lose heart, we lose motivation and when we lose motivation, we become overwhelmed with the empty feeling of not accomplishing what we set out to do. Nothing can be more discouraging than the feeling of being a failure, of not being able to finish something you started. You may have thought you had what it took to succeed, but then you became discouraged along the way and doubt set in. True winners, though, see failures only as temporary setbacks.

Fear

We can sometimes lose our sense of security because of fear. When we allow what other people say to produce fear, this in turn produces insecurity in us. We must be careful whom we listen to. Not everyone giving you advice is interested in your wellbeing and success. Fear can make us want to run away, but that's when we should remain immobile and not lose sight of our dreams.

I have been discouraged many times in my life and every time I am faced with a blow to my dreams, I am also faced with a blow to my self-esteem because the two are closely connected. That's when I have to decide to get back up again, dust myself off and try until I succeed (or at least get closure) and that's when my self-esteem grows. As you determine to get up every time you fall down, you are succeeding at something right there!

Joseph the Dreamer

Joseph's dream was tested, and so too will yours be. Your dream may suffer the test of familiarity — when people around are so familiar with what you are that they cannot see *who* you are. Don't let it affect you. Your dream may suffer the test of rejection, when people reject you because of your dream. Don't let it affect you. The test of distraction may disable your dream, when people try to pull you off the course of your dream.

Don't let them!

There's the test of confinement, when people try to box you into something that your dream wants to set you free from. Fight for your freedom. The test of time — hanging onto your dream for as long as it takes. Be patient. The test of self-doubt, when you question what you've actually dreamed. Remember the dream.

Finally, there's the test of grace, where you learn to appreciate the fulfillment of your dream without arrogance or pride, but with grace. Be grateful.

The rewards of being a dreamer can be astronomical! In the story *Joseph the Dreamer*, we see that he reaped the following rewards: influence, impact, prosperity, honor, favor, adventure and longevity. The same could be your rewards for daring to dream.

Joseph wasn't afraid to dream and he wasn't afraid to believe the dream, even when the circumstances were trying to play a different story. Joseph found himself in a pit and in prison before he finally reached the palace. If you are going to dream, you are going to have to take risks — it's all part of the process to seeing your dream fulfilled. You are also going to have to come to terms with the fact that not everyone will want to hear about your dream or see your dream fulfilled, especially if it means you will have some kind of 'advantage' over them.

Containment

Everyone feels contained at times. Sometimes this happens when we try to finish a task or accomplish something over and over with seemingly no success. Sooner or later we become discouraged and at some point we get so discouraged that we want to quit. This can happen with simple projects, education, and sometimes with a person's life.

A sense of containment can come at any time regardless of what great things we have accomplished already. You may feel as though you've had enough because you've been trying to do something for so long and now you feel you will never get it done. Abandonment may seem the only option, but abandonment will never see your dreams fulfilled.

Containment will make you think it is not worth it and this thinking affects our bodies, minds and emotions. Sometimes our feelings of containment can be so great that we neglect to do the simple necessities, such as eating properly. Another thing that might be neglected due to containment is taking care of basic everyday responsibilities. When we let things go undone, we wallow in our own self-pity and self-loathing. The feeling of containment may arise from various causes within ourselves, whether physical, mental or emotional, or from outside causes such as our circumstances, health, surroundings and associates.

Containment as a result of external factors can sneak up and bite hard. This could include financial loss or want, persecution, false accusations, and many other things that we may not be able to understand and which persist in crowding themselves into our everyday life.

When our dreams seem squashed within us, or taken away from us, that is the time to remember we do have control of what happens with our dream in the long run. Sometimes the battle is internal and your fight is with your own insecurities, doubts and poor choices, and other times the battle is on the outside from people who want to throw you in a pit to make sure your dreams never come true.

Regardless of the source, it's time to take back control. Your dreams can be successful regardless of what people and circumstances say, and you are the only one who can throw your dreams and self-esteem away.

Former British Prime Minister Sir Winston Churchill once said, 'Never give in — never, never, never, never, in nothing great or small, large or petty, never give in except to convictions of honor and good sense. Never yield to force; never yield to the apparently overwhelming might of the enemy.' Another great quote appears on the headstone of a remarkable woman who had suffered abuse at the hands of a loved one, and who had risen above the circumstances to confront the issue. It reads, 'The greatest success in life is not in never falling, but rising when you fall.'

We will all experience ups and downs, highs and lows, times of feeling elated and times of feeling deflated, as we pursue our dreams. Life is not just one big win, but it is a series of expansions and contractions. It is good to realize that you are not the only one who has suffered from containment and discouragement. Many people around you have probably already gone through similar circumstances. Seeing our pains and frustrations in the context of the suffering of those around us should help us to deal with our own weaknesses.

One thing that has the potential to hinder the progress of any dream is when we fail to relate to, or work well with other people. We need to work on relating more widely and effectively with people who have different ideas and viewpoints from our own. We need to try to understand what makes other people tick.

Another potential hindrance to seeing your dreams fulfilled is pride. Pride can definitely be part of the problem. When we think our dream is all that matters and we start bragging to people about what we are going to do and be, we won't necessarily find ourselves surrounded with people encouraging us.

A person who thinks they have 'arrived' can see no room in their lives for improvement. They are perfect in their own eyes. They feel and believe that no matter what comes against them they can't be conquered. This is a false sense of security and will lead to unbalanced and unhealthy self-esteem.

It can seem, with your life story, impossible to have or fulfill a dream. In the story *Joseph the Dreamer*, Joseph's life was one big accordion file, expanding and contracting with every dream he dreamed. It seemed that every time he dared to dream, someone or something was waiting to make sure he would never make it. But he saw the bigger picture — he saw the dream as a future reality.

You need to focus on the bigger picture of your life and aim to put everything you are going to do into some kind of context. If you are unable to do this yourself, get help from someone who can draw some healthy perspective from your life.

Ask yourself if what you are doing is going to take you closer to or further from your dream. A dream isn't a destination, it is a journey made up of mostly small choices.

Mistakes

If we choose to dream, sooner or later we will all fail at something. Failure is a universal experience that we risk if we allow ourselves to dream. There are people who have had more failures than successes, but those who are most devastated by their mistakes are those who think and believe that you can live life without ever making a single mistake.

We all make mistakes and experience setbacks, defeats and losses in life. We're all human and nobody's perfect. Our failures and defeats can have a devastating effect on our lives if not properly dealt with or handled with the right attitude and frame of mind.

Abraham Lincoln was well versed in failure before he took on his dream role as President of the United States of America:

★   He failed in business in 1831
★   He was defeated for legislature in 1832
★   He failed in business again in 1833
★   He suffered a nervous breakdown in 1836
★   He was defeated in his bid for speaker in 1838
★   He was defeated in his run for elector in 1840
★   He lost his bid for Congress in 1843
★   He lost his run for Senate in 1855
★   He was defeated in running for Vice President in 1856
★   He lost another run for Senate in 1858
★   He was elected President in 1860

The rest, as they say, is history!

When we feel defeated, we don't have to continue that way. We can conquer feelings of defeat and failure and move on to a brighter future if we learn how to get back up again when we've been knocked down.

In his book *Failing Forward*, bestselling author and motivational speaker on leadership, John Maxwell highlights the differentiation between average and achieving people. In his estimation, the major difference comes down to their perception of and response to failure.

Mistakes are a training process that we go through on our way to success. In other words, you and I are not going to succeed without making some mistakes along the way. The good news is that our mistakes do not have to be fatal or final. The problem with us is that we stop dreaming because we fear failure, and we cease believing in ourselves.

On a late night television program I once saw actor Harrison Ford being interviewed. He was discussing how he realized early on that success was tied to not giving up. In his experience, most people in the acting business gave up and went on to do other things. Hanging around long enough meant he was sure to outlast the people who arrived on the bus with him. I for one am glad he decided to hold onto that dream.

Don't be afraid to keep trying, and don't be afraid to make decisions for your life. If you make a wrong choice, then right the wrong and get on with it! You will never achieve anything you don't even attempt. Any movement forward — shuffle if you have to — is a step in the right direction. In other words, failure is a sure thing if you stop or never try. And don't be a perfectionist. If you want to please everyone along the way, you'll never succeed. It's just not possible to win at people pleasing. Someone, somewhere, in some way, will be disappointed with you and your dream.

Failing at accomplishing something does not make you a failure. What makes a person a failure is their refusal to get up and dream again. Henry Ford, the inventor of the Ford motor vehicle, once said, "Failure is merely an opportunity to begin again intelligently." World famous basketball player Michael Jordan once said, "I can accept failure. Everyone fails at something, but I can't accept not trying."

Down But Not Out

If you have already given up, then it's time to dream again. As long as you have breath, you have the opportunity to dream, and to live your dream. You may have been knocked down, but not out. Take one day at a time, and start by working with manageable tasks.

Remember that the fulfillment of your dream may also mean the fulfillment of another's dream, so please don't give up. Think about what would happen if you simply couldn't be bothered. When you get discouraged and depressed please don't allow yourself to become inactive and wallow in your own pity. Instead, follow some of the keys to freedom in this chapter, to help you see your dreams come alive.

The following are some suggestions to help you get back up and overcome discouragement in your life:

Rest and relax

Get some rest and relaxation! Sometimes the best thing to do when you are discouraged is to stop what you are doing and rest your body and mind. Often after a little rest and relaxation you can come back to the same task with a new approach. Eat right, sleep well, exercise and relax. Take some time off and get away from the things that are bringing you discouragement.

Reorganize

Get closure on some tasks. When you are discouraged, often it does not mean you're doing the wrong thing. It simply means maybe you're doing the right thing, but you're doing it in the wrong way. Don't give up on your dream, just reorganize and try a new approach.

Believe

Continue to believe and you will succeed! Make a list of all the things that have been good about life, all the things that have been positive. Count your blessings. Open up your eyes and see everything that you have already achieved. Look forward to the future and see everything you've promised yourself. Listen to the positive voices of people who encourage you to succeed and focus on their belief in you and your belief in yourself to achieve. Stare into the Mirror of Truth and believe in your dream.

Resist

In order to see your dream fulfilled, you need a plan. In order to succeed or accomplish anything, we must have a plan.

When we don't have a plan to follow we won't know where we are going or how we are going to get there.

Writing down your dreams and goals is an important first step towards achieving them. This will help you visualize your goals and commit to seeing them fulfilled. Although it is wonderful to dream, it is even better to actively commit yourself in both thought and deed.

Record your dreams with as much detail as possible so you can really visualize them. Do this for as many areas of your life as you can. Your dream could be about physical health, financial security or relational fruitfulness.

List the following:
* ★   The area that your dream is associated with (family, work, health)
* ★   The specific dream for that area
* ★   The steps you are taking to fulfill your dream.

Remember that the best way to make your dreams come true is to wake up! Dreams do not always stay the same, so update your goals as your dreams evolve. Perhaps you dream to live a long healthy life, or that you want to experience love and stay in love forever. It may be a dream to become a doctor or to return to school so you can get the degree you have longed for. It could be that you want to start a foundation or charity that helps others who are battling with issues you have been able to overcome. Maybe you want to write.

Remember too that you are never alone. There are always people who have experienced the same thing you are experiencing at your moment of discouragement. Think about those who push through. Their reward is the satisfaction of seeing their dream fulfilled. Stand firm and don't run! Don't give in to discouragement without a fight. Don't just roll over and give in. Resist it. Resist the discouragement. Remember your dream. Dream for you and dream for others who need to see your dream fulfilled. We are all at war with the negatives of life. You do not have to be discouraged. It is a choice. Don't give in and don't give up.

Never Give Up

Above my office desk is a large white blank canvas. It's intentionally blank, and I'm asked regularly if I intend to paint it sometime soon. The purpose of this lovely white canvas is to inspire me to dream. It reflects the commitment I have to myself to ensure that I flourish personally, even if my circumstances remain the same. I refuse to quit.

When I look into the potential of my blank canvas, I can be anyone I want to be and I can do anything I want to do — the sky is the limit.

I am a dreamer. I have many dreams and aspirations for my own life and for my family, and I was brought up to believe that I could achieve anything I put my heart and mind to. Your goals may be life-long, or they may be a result of a recent New Year's resolution. Whatever the case, you hold the key; it lies within your heart and mind. All it takes is an ordinary person with extraordinary perseverance to see a dream fulfilled.

I finished school after completing my School Certificate, at sixteen years old. The majority of my class left school at the same time, because only those wanting to go on to earn a degree at the university would need to stay. Times have now changed, and it has become increasingly important to finish your High School diploma, and preferably go on to get a college degree, if you want a good job.

Although I left school early and I don't hold a university degree, I have been able to see my dreams come true. It takes more than information and education to see your dreams come to pass. It takes tenacity and passion and a commitment not to give in to discouragement and self-pity, each time you go through hard times and it seems like you will never reach your goals.

I have some very specific goals, such as:
★   Enjoying married life, celebrating each year and reaching at least my fiftieth wedding anniversary.
★   Raising healthy, happy and flourishing children
★   Staying in shape for the rest of my life.
★   Writing a book every year for the rest of my life.
★   Using my life to help others live in freedom.

Obviously there are more, and these are just a sample of the kinds of things that are in the forefront of my mind when it comes to what I do every day. In order to achieve long-term dreams, we must make choices and take action every single day, in line with our dreams. It's the accumulation of those choices and actions which leads us to see our dreams become reality.

This book could have brought me much discouragement because it has taken me so long to finish it. Trying to find the time and brain space has caused it to take a lot more time and emotional energy than I thought it would. But, I refused to allow discouragement to set in. I had you in my sights. I had not only my dreams but also your dreams in mind. Your life and your self-esteem lay within my dream. My hope is that your dreams will be released because my dream has been released, and so the cycle of encouragement and fulfillment can go on.

Dare to Dream

Nelson Mandela once said, "We have laid the foundations for a better life. Things that were unimaginable a few years ago have become everyday reality."

For the unimaginable to become everyday reality, risks had to be taken. Every time we dream we take a risk. Just about anything that we do in life has some risk associated with it, and nothing of any value is ever accomplished without some kind of risk. This entails setting goals that require time, energy and passion to fulfill. Some people's goal is just to get out of bed in the morning and make it through the day just to go back to bed at night, with absolutely nothing accomplished in between. Where is the long-term life satisfaction in that?

We have to accept responsibility for our own lives. We are responsible for our actions, our words, our attitudes and our reactions toward others and life itself. We can't blame someone else for our shortcomings and downfalls in life, even though it's much easier to blame someone else. It's easy to make excuses as to why we failed or allowed ourselves to be defeated, rather than facing up to the truth.

Great accomplishments only come with great sacrifices. When we start something that requires more work, more energy, more time or more money than we anticipated, we should be inspired not to give up before we accomplish what we set out to do.

You can turn any adversity to your advantage if you approach it with the proper attitude and right frame of mind. For every negative experience we have there is a benefit to be had from it.

Oscar Wilde once said, "For a dreamer is one who can find his way by moonlight and see the dawn before the rest of the world." When you look at a seed, you can't see a tree — you can only see a seed. But you know within that seed is potentially a tree and an entire forest. This is the power of the dream within you, waiting to emerge. And within every dream lies another dream, waiting to come true. Dreamers need to stand the test of time. We need to learn that a delay in seeing our dreams fulfilled is not necessarily a denial of our dream happening.

It may appear at times that your dream is lost, but dreams don't ever really go away, unless you choose to throw them away. Choose to allow yourself to see your life as having three walls and a door setting you free, rather than four walls that say you will never see it happen for you.

Samuel Johnson once said, "It matters not how a man dies, but how he lives. The act of dying is not of importance, it lasts so short a time." This great man understood how important dreams are. Your dream is waiting to be birthed. Remember that even if there is a struggle for it to be realized, it does in fact exist, and is waiting for you to wake up and work on it.

Remember the Truth:
within every contraction lies the seed for an expansion.

10 keys to freedom

[from discouragement]

Freedom from discouragement is best done with encouragement and focusing on the future. Enjoy your dreams!

1.   Allow yourself to dream positive dreams.

2.   Believe that your dreams will come true. Write down your dreams and a plan for how you might achieve them.

3.   If you start to feel discouraged, don't allow discouragement to become a part of who you are. There is always hope!

4.   Don't ever give up.

5.   Express your dreams to those you can trust.

6.   Allow your dreams to unfold, rather than trying to make them happen through striving. Don't be impatient.

7.   Remain true to yourself and remain true to your dream, and you will eventually see your dream fulfilled.

8.   Don't doubt yourself.

9.   Keep a journal and look back through it from time to time so that you are careful not to miss it when it comes true.

10.   Be thankful for the ability to dream another dream.

body & soul
[action plan]

Body

Keep a record of your dreams, continually adding and updating them as you grow. Work on strategies, with help from others if necessary, to help see your dreams come true.

Soul

Cultivate dreams in your heart and continually give yourself permission to dream bigger dreams. Believe you will see your dreams come to pass in your lifetime, and that your dreams will be something to inspire the next generation.

**My goal is Freedom
FROM DISCOURAGEMENT**

my notes

[write your thoughts]

chapter twelve

Fully Amazing Grace

freedom from intimidation

["People do sometimes hurtful things when they are in pain."]

284 Mirror Mirror by Dianne Wilson

the slave trader

Once upon a time, there lived a boy whose mother loved him dearly. She taught him about good and evil, warning him to stay on the good path. His mother died when he was just seven years old, leaving his seaman father to care for the lad. By the age of eleven, the boy had accompanied his father on six voyages. When his father retired, the boy was transferred to a military ship where conditions were intolerable.

He fled the service, only to be captured and publicly beaten. After enduring flogging and demotion, he volunteered to transfer to a slave trading ship. His mother's words of advice forgotten, he chose this cruel occupation. He was angry at what life had dealt him so far. The slave trader with whom he worked brought him to his home in Africa to continue trading people for money. There, the trader's wife took pleasure in beating him every day.

His physical appearance changed. His posture and stance became hunched and withdrawn. Distraught, destitute and angry, the young man fled to the shoreline, where he built a fire to attract a passing ship. A ship finally saw the smoke and the skipper came ashore to rescue him.

He lived aboard for a long time. It was not uncommon for as many as 600 captives to be kept in the hold of this ship. One day, the young man's temper got him into trouble and he was beaten, thrown down below, and forced to live on rotten vegetables for an unendurable amount of time.

When the skipper brought him above to beat him again, the young man fell overboard. Because he couldn't swim, they harpooned him to pull him back onboard. Bleeding and defeated, he longed to be rescued.

Down below deck, like a ray of light, he remembered the words of his mother. He cried out for help, calling upon grace and mercy to deliver him. He heard murmurs from above, as a gentleman spoke with the captain of the ship. The captain came below the creaky deck and called the young man's name. "This fine sir just bought you to go and work with him." said the captain. As they left the ship, the gentleman turned toward the young man and said,

"You're free to go."

"What?" the young man asked.

"I was once set free and so I promised that I would help another poor wretch like me. Be on your way and remember the freedom you have received today so that one day you will grant freedom to someone else."

The young man walked away free, aware that he had inflicted much pain on people who didn't deserve it, robbing others of their dignity and freedom through trading in human suffering.

He came to his senses with deep sorrow for what he had done. He wrote about the rich mercy and grace given to him in the famous hymn "Amazing Grace." This is the legend of John Newton, a man whose life was turned around by grace. Once he had received the grace to start his life over again, he could not help but want to live a life showing grace and mercy towards others. And this became his happily ever after life.

the end

fact

Hurt people hurt people.

truth

Grace always overcomes hurt and intimidation.

mirror mirror on the wall ...

who can rescue me from myself?

One of the sad realities of life is that often people who have been hurt end up hurting others. Hurt people hurt people. When we are subject to another person's forceful will on our lives, intimidation can set in.

Everybody hurts somebody at some time or another. Most of us wish we could avoid hurting others. Yet some people hurt people repetitively, either intentionally or unintentionally, because of unresolved issues in their lives. These people usually lack empathy, healthy assertiveness and decision-making skills. They are also unable to manage their feelings adequately, generally have a low self-esteem and rarely feel they can understand themselves, let alone anyone else.

The presence of right and wrong has been on earth for a long time, and sometimes in our crazy, mixed-up world, it's difficult to decipher which is which. Something has to win in your life: either right or wrong, positive or negative, and no matter what has happened in your life up until now, it is entirely up to you to make the choice to live differently.

Intimidation

Intimidation is no stranger to anyone. Everybody can relate to what it feels like to be intimidated including experiences like the first day at school or work, or aggressive friends, peers, and bullies. Intimidation is a term I know well. Like many people, it is something that I have come up against time and time again throughout my life, and it's only been in more recent years that I have learned to resist and not succumb to the fear of another person ruling over my life.

To intimidate is defined as 'to make timid or fearful,' and fear itself is an intimidator! It happens when someone else threatens to use power or control to get others to do what they want them to do or to prevent them from doing what that individual is about to do. It also happens when someone makes themselves out to be more powerful or forceful than they really are, and when they use coercion or force to get what they want from others, or to cause others to shrink. When people use verbally, physically, sexually or emotionally abusive behaviors to get other people to stay in line, that is considered intimidation. Intimidation can come from people, situations, gatherings and the unknown. Intimidation occurs when someone acts in such a way that no one would dare question or stand up to them over any of their decisions, opinions or directives, or when they convince others that only they have enough experience, wisdom, intellect and insight to give direction or to have the correct answers to life's problems.

If someone uses physical size, stature and strength to get others to respect and obey them, it is intimidation. Intimidation comes in many forms, but it is always ugly.

The primary purpose of intimidation is to keep us "in line" or "in a box," and the moment we dare to move outside the line or the box, we are likely to be on the receiving end of anger and more intimidation. Intimidation is definitely one of life's big "nasties" that seeks primarily to distract, discourage and hurt. It needs identifying and eradicating in order for you to develop healthy self-esteem.

Intimidators have learned that intimidation works. They do it to feel powerful and in control. There are things you can do to deal with the situation without making things worse.

The facts are:
★ Intimidators keep intimidating as long as it works, and as long as it makes them feel more powerful.
★ Intimidation takes lots of forms: it can be physical, verbal or emotional, ranging from mild to severe.
★ Women can be intimidators, although intimidation by women is more likely to be expressed by spreading rumors, leaving people out of social events, or threatening to withdraw friendship, rather than of a physical nature.

Anyone can be the target of intimidation. Most victims often feel less powerful than the person intimidating them, therefore a typical victim is likely to be shy, sensitive and perhaps anxious or insecure.

Some people are picked on for physical reasons, such as being overweight or small, wearing different clothing, having a physical disability, or belonging to a different race or religious faith. Some intimidators are outgoing, aggressive, active and expressive. They get their way by brute force or openly harassing someone. They may even carry a weapon. This type of intimidator rejects rules and regulations and needs to rebel to achieve a feeling of being better than everyone else.

Other intimidators are more reserved and sly and may not want to be seen as harassers or tormentors. They try to control by talking, saying the right thing at the right time, and lying. This type of intimidator gets their power secretively through manipulation and deception. As different as these types may seem, intimidators do have some characteristics in common:

★ They focus on their own pleasure.
★ They want power and control over others.
★ They are willing to use and abuse other people to get what they want.
★ They find it difficult to see things from someone else's perspective.

The negative effects of intimidation are many. People who choose to use fear and intimidation to control others will soon find themselves facing emotional barriers in relationships, and they will also risk being seen as emotionally, verbally, physically and even perhaps sexually abusive in their dealings with other people.

I have come to realize first-hand, that hurt people hurt people, and therefore if I look deeply at why someone is angry, hurting or intimidating towards me, I can see that they, more than likely, have been subject to another person's anger, hurt and intimidation. As a result, this becomes a learned art as the intimidator doesn't know any better, and the cycle continues, or stops, with me. Understanding why people intimidate doesn't excuse the act, it simply explains it. Don't get dragged into the 'I don't know any better, so it's okay' game.

Intimidation is a twofold issue. There is the intimidator and the person receiving the intimidation. Both people will suffer a blow to their identity and will need help developing a healthy self- esteem again. If you have been subjected to intimidation, you will have possibly found it difficult reading this chapter so far. Much of it may seem far too real to you, especially if you are currently in a situation where you are suffering intimidation. While there are varying degrees of intimidation, any of it, in any form is wrong and destructive to the human soul.

No matter what kind of intimidation and hurt I have been subjected to, I refuse to pass that pain on to other people, whether they deserve it or not. That's where I win! I get to choose my future, my friendships, and where my boundaries are set.

The Slave Trader

In *The Slave Trader,* John Newton found it difficult coping with the death of his mother at the tender age of seven. Through intense grief, he ended up making decisions that would steer his destiny away from good, into a life of pain, suffering and loss of self-respect and self-esteem.

John set his life on a path of self-destruction when he ignored his conscience and gave his life over to angry and hurtful living. The more he hurt himself and others, the worse his self-esteem became. When he eventually looked into the mirror of truth, he saw what he really looked like: a wretched man. His self-esteem was as low as it could possibly be, and he dealt with his pain by inflicting pain on others. He treated others with no respect or dignity, because of his own lack of self-respect and dignity.

The slaves aboard John Newton's ship were forcibly and physically enslaved, and you may feel as though that is exactly what your life has become — enslaved by certain circumstances in your life. It doesn't have to stay this way — you do have some control. It may only be a little control at first, but it can grow to a point where you are able to free yourself from the things that you feel intimidate you. Eventually, John Newton saw what a mess his life had become, and he recognized that it was up to him to take personal responsibility for it.

Although he was a victim of his circumstances in the beginning of his life, he had now grown up and he needed to stop blaming the world for what had happened to him, in order to start building his life again. He had a reputation for destroying people's lives, when he could have become a builder of people's lives. People do strange things when they are in pain, and the younger the person, the more challenging it is to negotiate through the haze of pain.

the intimidator

On the other hand, if you have been able to identify yourself as an intimidator, and you wish to change your behavior, then you will need to take action.

1.   Ask people in your life if they find you intimidating.

2.   Find out what it is about you that they find intimidating (your words, your actions, etc.).

3.   Ask yourself if you can now see these character traits and whether they have been intentional or unintentional.

4.   Take a long hard look at the negative consequences of your intimidation, whether intentional or not.

5.   Think about the irrational and unhealthy causes for your thinking and beliefs that may have contributed to you intimidating other people.

6.   Identify healthy, rational and positive thinking and beliefs that will help to contribute to you ceasing to intimidate in the future.

7.   Specify how you will intentionally behave in the future.

8.   Decide what you can do to lessen any intimidating effects you have on others.

9.   Speak up and assure those you've hurt that you no longer intend to intimidate them, and ask them for their continued constructive feedback.

10.   Start acting on your new positive choices and monitor responses from people in your world.

Rather than maintaining his life of torment, John Newton cried out for help to get off the roller coaster of destruction. He finally came to his senses and saw what his life had become, all because he hadn't dealt with his pain in a constructive way.

Yet after inflicting so much pain on himself and others, it was going to take a miracle for him to forgive himself and have a new start in life. Receiving grace gave John a new approach and a new appearance. He not only was different on the inside, it showed on the outside through his actions and bearing. The life and joy that once was lost in him was found again. The light that shone through the crack in the ship's deck brought truth and meaning to John's life. Light can either lead us and guide us or blind us; it's up to us to choose.

Anger

Inside the heart of the intimidator is a seed of anger that flares and flourishes if it is fed. Unhealthy anger is the fuel that keeps the cycle of intimidation going. When we look at angry behavior we can see there are different types of anger and consequences that come with each of them.

Bullying behavior causes fear and results in intimidation, hurting both the victim and the bully. Bullying is repeated and uncalled-for aggressive behavior, or quite simply, unprovoked meanness. It's a form of intimidation, designed to threaten, frighten, or get someone to do something they would not ordinarily do.

If a child experiences constant intimidation, they may learn to expect this kind of behavior from others. They may develop a pattern of giving in to the unfair demands of the intimidator, and they may end up identifying with the bully and become a bully themselves — all from a position of fear and intimidation.

We know that the bully or intimidator is also hurt in the process, and if they are allowed to continue the behavior, it becomes habitual.

They become more likely to surround themselves with friends who condone their aggressive behavior, and they may never truly develop a mature sense of what is right and wrong. Bullies or intimidators do not go away when school ends. The behavior continues through high school and even into adulthood. It can lead to serious problems and dangerous situations for both the victim and the aggressor.

Aggressive anger drives one person to hurt another physically, emotionally or psychologically. It is usually expressed by hitting, kicking, harassing, using put-downs and threatening, and sometimes can even result in killing. When someone is aggressively angry, they are well aware of that fact, so they try to make someone else accountable by blaming and avoiding responsibility. This type of anger is typical of men who abuse their partners.

Another form of anger is *passive–aggressive*, which is internalizing and denying, and is usually expressed by silence, revenge, rumor starting and depression. When bottled up, it will eventually blow up aggressively. The person who is passively angry denies what's going wrong and doesn't want to communicate.

Assertive anger is expressed in non-threatening ways that do not hurt you, another person or property. This form of anger is dealt with by suppression and by acknowledging the feeling and by making the decision to deal with the situation at a more appropriate time in the near future. This kind of self-control speaks of a strong self-esteem and it is the type of anger that is actually considered healthy. An example of this is when we choose to confront an issue that has made us angry, but in a constructive and calm way — without losing it!

People can't *make* you angry. You have the power to choose the feelings you have and power to decide what to do with those feelings in any situation. There is healthy and unhealthy anger, and we can choose to deal with any anger in a way that will either harm or heal and include or reject others.

Besides the physical signs we sense in our body telling us we are feeling angry, there are other signs or triggers we can learn to understand in order to take charge of our anger:

★ **External Triggers**
These are the things that are done to us.
★ **Internal Triggers**
These are the messages we tell ourselves that get us all worked up.

When you are feeling angry, recognize why you are angry and try to calm down. Take a deep breath and don't speak. If need be, leave the situation until you can handle it constructively. It's vital that you consider the consequences that come with your response to anger and remember, your response is your choice.

Eleanor Roosevelt once said, "No one can make you feel inferior without your consent." And, no one can make you angry, intimidated or fearful without your consent.

Control

Intimidation is a control issue because it is the attempt of one person to coerce others into doing what they want them to do, and it usually involves control strategies such as threats, pressure, physical force and power plays. If you don't do what they say, they will try to make you do it or if you don't agree with what they say, they will try to make you agree with them. It's all about their control of you.

If you intimidate another person, it robs them of their free choice and free will, and it makes another person a victim of your control and needs. This is a violation of their will. It is in no way acceptable to build your own self-esteem by willfully destroying another's. When you lord it over another person with an angry spirit, you weaken the will in those who feel beaten down, abused and oppressed.

Control comes about through irrational thinking — thoughts like, "I will use whatever it takes to get my way," or "No one will ever get away without showing respect for my authority." Controllers believe that the more they control people, the more they will get out of them. The more "respect" they receive, the more they will be obeyed. They love to remind others of how much they have done for them, and they think that the only way to get anything done is to beat people down until they can take it no more.

Enough is Enough

Allowing yourself to believe you are worth something is the first step in the right direction towards helping you get you out from under intimidation.

Following the steps or path out is crucial, as is making a commitment to yourself to accept that there may be unwanted consequences to freeing yourself up from the intentional or unintentional intimidation of this person. This may mean the end of a relationship.

Intimidation Action Plan

In order for you to get out from under another person's intimidation, you will need to take some action for yourself, as follows:

1. First, you need to recognize if you are being or have been intimidated, which means no more living in denial of the facts.

2. Write down when you were or are being intimidated, and list the people who have in the past or currently do intimidate you.

3. Be specific with what it is they have used to intimidate you.

4. Identify whether the intimidation has been intentional (in their control) or unintentional (possibly outside their control).

5. Identify how long you have been suffering intimidation with each person.

6. List how your being intimidated has affected your relationship with the person.

7. Identify how much of the intimidation you have allowed to affect you because of your own unhealthy beliefs and thoughts about yourself.

8. Change your posture. Stand tall and don't cower.

9. Change your voice. Be calm but firm, and audible.

10. Use eye contact. Don't stare at the ground or the sky. Look people in the eye, remembering that they are human, just like you, and you have nothing to be afraid of.

Think practically when it comes to breaking out from under intimidation. Spend time with bigger people, and don't shrink back. Do something that you wouldn't normally do to challenge fear in your life. Talk to someone whom you would normally try to avoid. If your circumstances are extreme, you will need to take action to lessen the power of the person who is intimidating you by removing yourself from their presence, if at all possible. This may mean more responsibility will be required from you to carry your share of making the relationship healthy.

You will then be ready to behave in a new and less intimidated way. As time passes, you need to continually tell yourself that you are worthwhile. I don't think there's anything wrong with talking to yourself. I do it often! I'd rather chat away to myself and reinforce positive things I know need to be said, than sitting or sulking in silence waiting to receive affirmation from other people in order to know who I am and how valuable I am. Tell yourself that you are valuable and deserve better. Remind yourself that we are all equal and therefore you don't need to see others as better than you. As you take more control over and responsibility for your life, you will also become naturally more positively assertive. Once you know better, no one will be able to hold intimidation over you unless you allow them.

Identity

I've been intimidated many times in my life, by bosses, business people and family members, but I choose now to believe I am worth something. I have learned it doesn't really matter who or what intimidates you. It could be a store associate or a school principal, a work colleague or even your spouse. Even if the cause is external, the solution isn't. It's internal. Some things we have to work on from within and they may take us all of our lives and into eternity.

When we feel intimidated by another person, internally we're viewing others and ourselves in a kind of pecking order. In other words, we are at the bottom of the food chain, less important, significant or valuable than others.

We can sometimes think, "You're important, therefore I am not," and "You are worthwhile, therefore I am not." These thoughts become reality if we choose to give them life by thinking about them and believing them. You may think others are richer, more beautiful, smarter, more important or more popular. The list will be as long as our insecurities are deep. But in all of these scenarios, we are viewing life in only one limited, false dimension. We're adopting an incorrect view of ourselves and others, and we're not seeing the truth.

Having a handle on intimidation doesn't mean you won't be subjected to anyone's poor behavior towards you in the future. It just means you are now aware and skilled in how to deal with their intimidation and your responses. Fears and hurts will still come, but you don't have to live afraid and in pain.

There are many forms of fear, and they are generally categorized into phobias. My natural tendency is towards fear and anxiety. I was a reasonably anxious child, and I internalized most of my fears because I was simply too afraid to express them. When I became an adult, I found that the fears that I didn't deal with when I was younger just grew with me and they then became adult fears. Because of my naturally fearful nature, I succumbed easily to intimidation.

Some of my phobias were fear of spiders (arachnophobia) and flying, and there were many, many more. My grandmother suffered from telephonophobia, or a fear of the telephone! I had so many fears that I had phobophobia, which is the fear of fear!

Grace to Forgive

Whenever intimidation is present, grace is absent. Grace is the glue that holds together a broken life. But grace must be appropriated, that is, you must first receive it to be able to live it and then, in turn, give it.

In his book *The Grace Awakening*, author Charles R. Swindoll says:
We use grace to describe many things in life:
★ A well-coordinated athlete or dancer
★ Good manners and being considerate of others
★ Beautiful, well-chosen words
★ Consideration and care for other people
★ Various expressions of kindness and mercy

So, what really is grace? It is truly something that is represented here in the story *Amazing Grace*, and in each of the stories in this book.

Without grace, people in trouble cannot pick themselves up off the floor and get on with life, no matter how hard they try. Grace is a gift from above, it doesn't actually come from within, and that's where most people go wrong.

When we feel that we can live life on our own, by ourselves, without anything or anyone to help us, that's when we make the first big mistake. We need grace to move beyond our mistakes and failings and to pick us up when we fall down.

When someone has been through a tragedy and can't seem to get over it, whether it has been self-inflicted or inflicted on them by someone else, the absence of grace in their life will prevent them from being free. Grace is active forgiveness, where you choose not to bring up the past against yourself or another person. Grace is absolutely and totally free. You will never be asked to pay it back. No one ever could, even if they tried.

Where someone has a lack of grace, they also usually have:

★   A lack of love and care for themselves and others
★   Rationalization for a life of doing their own thing, regardless of whom it hurts
★   Unwillingness to be accountable to anyone
★   Resistance to anyone getting close
★   Disregard for wise advice

The *Oxford Dictionary* definition of forgiveness is 'to remit, to let somebody off a debt, to cease to resent, pardon, and wipe the slate clean.'

This is what John Newton experienced.

Forgiveness, like love, is a decision. Forgiveness takes courage and determination. No one can make you feel bad. You have the power to choose between becoming bitter or getting better. Take responsibility for your feelings; claim your power. Forgiveness takes practice. Start with small hurts and work your way up to the big ones. People hurt each other because they are learning and growing. Forgive people for their incompleteness and their humanness. If you find it hard to forgive your parents for their imperfect parenting, remember, they were shaped by the imperfect parenting they received from their parents, and so on.

Forgive yourself for what you regret doing and for what you wish you had done. Forgive yourself for not being fully yourself and for being only yourself. Forgiving yourself cleanses the soul and gives you the power to extend forgiveness to others.

Forgiveness is not something you do for someone else; it is something you do for yourself. Give yourself the gift of forgiveness.

Forgiving others is the first grace key, and then forgiving yourself and allowing yourself to have a new start is the second grace key in your life.

To live a life of grace means that you will be able to:

★   Live without being bound by impulses
★   Be free to make your own choices
★   Not live comparing yourself to others
★   Live a self-controlled existence
★   Fast-track your growth towards greater maturity and freedom, to be the person you were born to be

The single most powerful thing about grace is when we can accept it for ourselves. You can't give grace unless you have first received it for yourself. That's when you can know a fresh, new start for your life. My dream and hope for you is that you come to realize that it is impossible to fall from grace; you have to jump.

Remember the Truth:
grace always overcomes hurt and intimidation.

grace

★ The act of showing favor or kindness to someone who doesn't deserve it

★ Being forgiven for something you've done to hurt someone else

★ The act of forgiving someone for something they have done to hurt you

★ Something that's given and received, not earned

amazing grace

Amazing grace, how sweet the sound,
That saved a wretch like me.
I once was lost but now am found,
Was blind, but now I see.
'Twas grace that taught my heart to fear,
And grace, my fears relieved.
How precious did that grace appear
the hour I first believed.
Through many dangers, toils and snares,
We have already come.
'Twas grace that brought us safe thus far,
And grace will lead us home.

John Newton
1725–1807

10 keys to freedom

[from intimidation]

These keys are quick to read but may take a long time to implement. Forgiveness in particular is a long-term process, so be patient and press on with it.

1.   Ask forgiveness from those you have wronged. Knowing you have a clean slate will help you start afresh.

2.   Forgive others. This also helps clear the slate and lets you feel like you have a new start.

3.   Forgive yourself. This can be harder than the first two. Just know that you are no different from others — you need forgiveness from yourself too.

4.   Be slow to judge and quick to love.

5.   Realize that you are powerless to change without grace.

6.   Accept grace with open arms.

7.   Realize that healthy self-esteem comes from living a grace life.

8.   Don't dwell on it, but do remember where you came from and the mess your life was once in.

9.   Give grace to others.

10. Use your life story to help others.

body & soul

[action plan]

Body

Count to ten before you open your mouth, and try not to speak through your anger. Wait until you have calmed down enough to communicate constructively.

Soul

Don't let the sun go down on your anger. Resolve issues before you go to sleep, for the sake of peace and well-being. Believe for the ability to remain calm in the midst of turmoil and to deal positively with situations that make you angry or frustrated, and ask quickly for forgiveness — life's too short!

**My goal is Freedom
FROM INTIMIDATION**

my notes

[write your thoughts]

conclusion

A New Perspective

the next level

The truth that leads to change is confronting.

liᏒe

Life is an opportunity, benefit from it.
Life is beautiful, admire it.
Life is bliss, taste it.
Life is a dream, realize it.
Life is a challenge, meet it.
Life is a duty, complete it.
Life is a game, play it.
Life is a promise, fulfill it.
Life is sorrow, overcome it.
Life is a song, sing it.
Life is a struggle, accept it.
Life is a tragedy, confront it.
Life is an adventure, dare it.
Life is too precious, do not destroy it.
Life is life, fight for it.

Mother Teresa of Calcutta

mirror mirror on the wall ...
how do I find meaning to it all?

In the previous twelve chapters, I have endeavored to tackle some of life's most crippling issues that can lead to a destroyed, or at least damaged, identity. I have written about the problems and then offered some practical solutions. Yes, there is much we can do on our own to change our lives through positive thinking and practical behavioral changes, but the next level in attaining a healthy and most desirable self-esteem is through our lives being connected to a higher purpose.

I believe that it is this level that will touch the very heart of your innermost need to be loved and to feel valued, and will set you far apart from your problems.

Mother Teresa is an amazing example of someone who lived life for a purpose greater than herself. She lived her life for others. Mother Teresa gave her life to dignify people in their darkest hours, to help them die knowing they were loved. She knew who she was, and understood why she was here. She had an amazing outlook on life. When we have healthy self-esteem, we are able to live beyond ourselves and start to help others in their life journey. In this conclusion, I want to equip you with practical tools for continued motivation and lasting change in your own life, to start living a life that positively impacts the world around you.

Whenever you are feeling left out, unattractive, stupid, self-conscious, misunderstood, outcast, abused, useless, worthless and forgotten, remember what has been reflected in the Mirror of Truth about you.

you are

You are unique
You are beautifully and wonderfully made
You are special
You are priceless
You are valuable
You can be anything you want to be
You are a winner
You are not alone
You are a champion
You are beautiful
You are you!

Motivation

Motivation isn't only about encouraging people to improve for improvement's sake, it's about presenting a powerful reason for immediate action and giving clear responsibility to people for their own life. It is about knowing what is going to move you to action and using that knowledge to create confidence and commitment. Motivation is about painting a vivid and compelling picture of what is possible if you dare to change.

Robert Hriegel and David Brandt in their book *Sacred Cows Make the Best Burgers* give four keys to creating motivation to change things in your life:

1. Urgency
2. Inspiration
3. Ownership
4. Rewards

I have adapted these four keys to self-esteem as follows:

1. Urgency

A sense of urgency can be enough motivation to change something in your life. You can feel bad about yourself and know you want change, but urgency will give you the motivation to make those changes NOW. Urgency doesn't wait for tomorrow's answers, it doesn't need someone else's permission and its entire energy operates from the thought "I NEED to do it and I need to do it NOW!" You can help create a sense of urgency by gathering people around you who will motivate you. These people book you into the beauty salon for that facial you have always wanted, the haircut you've always shied away from and they don't listen to you ALWAYS talking about how you are going to change things. They say "Why wait? Do it now!" They also help you implement a plan to achieve those changes and are mature enough to stop you from becoming unhealthily obsessive about the whole process.

2. Inspiration

Urgency lights the fire. It creates the spark, producing the attitude and atmosphere needed to get you motivated to change. It is urgency that creates an adrenaline burst of action — like when you decided to join the gym perhaps. But this spark will definitely burn out if it is not stoked, and that's where inspiration comes in. We need a cause, not just a vision for your life. It's not enough for you to feel the need to change, you need direction on where the change is going to take you. You need to aspire to greater heights and go beyond previous limitations. You need passion and enthusiasm for your future. Who do you want to be and how are you going to become that person?

3. Ownership

Ownership is very attractive, as it not only gives you control over your own destiny, but you reap all the benefits life produces. Giving responsibility for your life and self-esteem over to your circumstances is throwing away a great opportunity for you to personally reap these ownership rewards. You need to be empowered with information and then be responsible with your actions; you will then be personally accountable for the results received.

4. Rewards

The best way to motivate you to get excited about your plans to change is by focusing on the rewards. If you sow well, you will reap well. If you sow negatively, you will reap negatively. There are different types of rewards — some external, some internal:

★ External: *Body*

If you eat properly, exercise regularly and take care of your physical appearance, you will reap external rewards, such as great health.

★ Internal: *Soul*

If you address areas of your mind (thinking), will (that potentially stubborn side of you) and emotions that may be holding you back from who you are really meant to be, then you will reap internal rewards, such as being in control of your thoughts and emotions.

The motivation for making these changes should come from within. When you are really ready for change, the sense of urgency should lead to inspiration, then personal responsibility (ownership), and it is then that you will reap great rewards.

As I have said before, the truth that leads to change is confronting. You must be prepared to declare war on those things that are enemies to your self-esteem and preventing you from living a life of true freedom.

Where there is a lack of freedom, there is usually a lack of self-esteem and the absence of true identity. In war, the sacrifice of life will result in the freedom of people, so too in life is pain almost always the price of freedom and liberty.

You may feel as though your life began downtrodden, without hope of a better future, or you may have grown up in an environment of fear and uncertainty, living in a state of oppression. It is time to stand up, declare war and fight for your freedom.

War is the time to fight and not the time to bow down to the enemy. Your enemy may be an eating disorder, or a battle with the mirror over your body image, or an addiction, bad habit, poverty, or a destructive relationship. Whatever the enemy of your life, you need to fight for freedom. The enemy will not go away — you can choose to ignore it, but it will still be there as its eradication does not depend on you choosing not to see it; its death comes in you seeing it and dealing with it — just as in real war. That results in true freedom.

True freedom is also not simply a matter of doing your own thing. True freedom exists within healthy boundaries.

If your freedom is important to you right now, look up at the sky and dream about growing wings to fly. Your freedom is a major key in the healthy development of your self-esteem. It will allow you to feel confident and empowered to live the life you were created to live.

Remember that a desirable life is one of freedom, not perfection. It is my desire that having read this book you will have gained the confidence and tools to shake off self-consciousness, develop a genuine sense of who you really are, and enjoy an inner confidence that will enable you to live out your dreams.

To love ourselves and to love other people properly, we need to be confident. The person with healthy self-esteem will treat others with respect. To love yourself isn't to be vain or self-indulgent, but rather to have a healthy appreciation for who you are and how you are made.

Stand tall, hold your head up and enjoy your new life of freedom. Know the TRUTH and the TRUTH will set you free.

You are worth it!

mirror, mirror

Mirror, mirror on the wall,
Who's the fairest of them all?
You are, of course!
Why can't you see?
Just be the best that you can be.
Discover the truth inside my frame,
And see your worth and value named.
Hope, truth, grace and freedom bound
The true you is set at last to be found.

freedom steps

Take some of these freedom steps and step into a future that you were designed for.

1. Believe and have faith in your heart that you can and will be free.

2. Practice positive thinking, seeing and doing.

3. Don't allow your thinking to be boxed in and confined.

4. Write a list of what you want freedom from.

5. Set some healthy boundaries for your life, and don't cross them.

6. Look up at the sky and see how expansive your world of opportunity is.

7. Next time you see a bird flying, remind yourself that you can do the same, here on earth.

8. Be kind to people in your world and allow them to be free in your presence.

9. Fight for what is good and right, without ever hurting anyone else.

10. Never, ever, ever, ever give up until you are free.

my notes

[write your thoughts]

action plan

Creative Journaling

it's my life

For us to like and feel comfortable with ourselves, it is important that we receive constant positive input. Children look to their parents to build their egos and self-esteem, so they can feel valuable and important. However, sometimes parents become so busy and overwhelmed by life's pressures, they may not say or do the best things to build the self-esteem of their children, and they may well be struggling with their own emotional problems and lack of self-esteem.

There is no doubt that lack of positive feedback and reinforcement undermines how we feel about ourselves as we are growing up. If we are continually corrected and told what is wrong with us and in need of improvement, our sense of identity will not be given the boost we need. Negative reinforcement is fertile ground for low self-esteem, and the reality is we all need encouragement and reassurance.

We need to know that we are thought of as valued, capable, worthwhile human beings.

To help log your journey of building your self-esteem, I suggest you keep a journal to start expressing yourself — your successes, achievements, goals, dreams and hopes for your life. As you put pen to paper, I believe you will begin to feel a real sense of ownership for your life and growing self-esteem.

Journals are powerful as they keep account of your life. On the following pages you'll find a 21-day guide to help you get started in your own personal journaling process.

21-Day Creative Journaling

As it generally takes three weeks to break and make a habit, I have devised a 21-day journal for you to follow to increase your self-esteem.

I suggest you begin by starting with just one poor habit that is damaging your self-esteem and work on that habit until the twenty-one days are up. Then, on the twenty-second day, start with the next bad habit and replace it with the opposite, positive action and create for yourself a brand new good habit. You may have many bad habits that have lowered your self-esteem, such as:

★   Negative self-talk
★   Nail biting and lip biting
★   Poor thoughts about yourself
★   Fear of taking risks
★   Presuming the worst

I have created twenty-one keys for you to follow on the twenty-one days you work at breaking any negative identity cycle you may be living with. Try these suggestions and see what happens. There are many more things that you can do.

Let me know how these things work out for you — I would love to hear your story. As you follow each day and keep a journal, your progress — as you challenge yourself and change — will encourage you to continually work towards a healthier self-esteem and identity.

Day 1
All of our efforts are a success if we learn from them.
What effort have you made today towards developing a healthier self-esteem?

Day 2
Courage comes from trying something new.
What new thing have you tried today?

Day 3
You have not because you ask not.
What do you want out of life today, next year and by the time you retire — relationally, emotionally, financially? Set some short- and long-term goals.

Day 4
Being able to enjoy your own company is great.
What good things have you learned about yourself when you are on

your own?

Day 5
Most people aren't necessarily doing better than you.
Make an honest list of all the people who are genuinely doing better than you and write down why.

Day 6
Accepting yourself the way you are is a great place to start.
List everything you cannot change about yourself and include a positive comment about each.

Day 7
Opportunities happen all day long and are nothing to be afraid of.
What were the opportunities you took today?

Day 8
You may feel you are not as attractive, intelligent and well off as most people.
List at least three positive qualities you have in relation to your looks, your intellect and your finances.

Day 9
Listen to your inner voice.
What positive things did your inner voice have to say today?

Day 10
If you sow energy, you will reap energy.
Make an exercise plan and make it part of your life, starting today!

Day 11
A healthy eating plan will make you feel fantastic.
Find a great eating plan suitable to your lifestyle and make the necessary changes starting from today.

Day 12
We all have reason to be proud of some things in our lives.

What are you proud of?

Day 13
Love and respect flourish when reciprocated.
How did you show love and respect today?

Day 14
Friendliness attracts friends.
What positive thing did you do today to attract a friend?

Day 15
The thoughts that you feed yourself on a regular basis strongly influence your self-esteem.
List the positive thoughts you had about yourself today.

Day 16
You are more successful than you think.
Boost your self-esteem by making a list of your successes.

Day 17
We can all improve who we are.
What did I do today to improve myself?

Day 18
You won the sperm race from around 600 million competitors!
Write down everything you have won at, including your conception and birth.

Day 19
Everyone's good at something.
List all of your gifts, talents and strengths.

Day 20
Everyone needs encouragement to flourish.
Write down the encouraging comments you received and gave today.

Day 21
Try and try again and don't give up until you have a breakthrough.

322   Mirror Mirror by Dianne Wilson

Write down everything you have had a breakthrough in, after not giving up.

Your self-esteem journal will prove a useful tool if you are honest, consistent and kind to yourself. In due course, you will reap the benefits of healthier self-esteem. Now that you have built up a list of positive commentary about your life, read it often. Read it when you are up, and you'll feel even better. Read it when you are down and you'll get a boost (and a kick in the pants for any negativity that may have crept in!). As your healthy self-esteem grows, and it will grow more and more each day, keep writing in your journal and enjoy your new life — you deserve it.

my identity creed

I value myself for seeing the positive lessons in what appeared to be a negative situation.

I value myself for doing what was fearful.

I can always do it afraid.

I value myself for getting out of a bad situation by making some difficult decisions.

I value myself for making positive changes in my life.

I value myself for being willing to remove walls and to establish safe boundaries in my life.

I value myself for risking new things.

I value myself for engaging in a healing process.

I value myself for letting go of the past.

I value myself for getting this far on the journey and not giving up.

I value myself because I am wonderfully made.

an expert opinion

Beliefs and Behavior

What the Doctor Says

I met with psychologist Dr. Vivienne Riches while researching this book. I found what she had to say very valuable and helpful and so I have included it for your interest.

In her practice Dr. Riches uses a method called cognitive behavioral therapy to help people with poor self-esteem and body image issues. Behavioral therapy is a method previously recognized as useful, and more recently a blend of behavioral and cognitive therapy has proven valid.

Original Behavioral Model

Based on the premise that a change in consequences/results leads to a change in behavior; it does not challenge the beliefs and therefore won't break some cycles.

A	B	C
Antecedent	**Behavior**	**Result**
E.g. a situation where two kids have one toy	One child hits the other to obtain the toy	The one who hits gets away with it!

Cognitive Behavioral Model

Enables you to change the result, and end the cycle, by challenging the beliefs.

A	B1	C
Antecedent	**Beliefs**	**Result**
E.g. a situation where two kids have one toy	Automatic thought of one child to hit the other. They believe if they don't hit, they won't get the toy. Their evaluation is based on irrational beliefs: 'If I don't hit, I won't get the toy,' or, 'It's OK to hit to get what I want. I want what I want now.'	The one who hits doesn't get away with it!

B2
Feelings
The hitting child is challenged about their auto response, and given 'healthy' options to obtain the toy or even to wait or share a toy.

B3
Behavior
The hitting child understands it is wrong to hit to get their own way, and so their thinking, feeling and behavior change.

Through cognitive behavioral therapy, repetitive destructive patterns can be found and challenged. This is achieved by first understanding that there is a problem, rather than living in denial or ignoring issues, hoping that they will go away, because they won't. The next step is to get in touch with the irrational thoughts and learn how to challenge them.

Dr. Riches says that the downside of cognitive behavioral therapy is that it doesn't highlight the human will. She believes that to activate the will is to activate the end solution. In other words, all the therapy in the world, be it behavioral or cognitive behavioral, won't lead anyone into freedom without their will being involved.

To activate a person's will, they must first understand that they can choose to do this. Many people don't understand that they are fully in charge of their will. Where there is a will, there is absolutely a way — to freedom! Once the person's will is activated, a new realm of possibilities is unlocked, where previously the destructive and repetitious behavior would have prevailed.

Exercising the will enables people to overcome habits of negative thinking and behavior. This cannot be achieved by force, it can only be achieved by the activation of one's will. For someone who has been engaging in destructive thinking and behavior for many years, the process of activating their will in a positive sense is usually difficult to establish. The way forward is to start by speaking kindly to oneself and to concentrate on one kind thought and word a day until the will begins to 'kick in.'

In twenty-one years of practice, Dr. Riches has spent many thousands of hours counseling patients and she believes whole-heartedly in therapy that covers not only behavior and thinking, but also the belief system of a person's life. The belief system relates to issues of the heart and relationships. In her practice she has only ever come across two patients who weren't interested in the health of their belief systems.

When asked about how she would take someone with low self-esteem to a healthy self-esteem, Dr. Riches mentioned the following three steps:

★ Behavioral
★ Cognitive
★ Belief

Dr. Riches usually starts talking to people about their childhood, because most times this is where the belief system is established: through the family of origin and schooling. Then, the process covers understanding how you feel about yourself, the world, and coping with life.

Beliefs are laid down in pain, so conditions such as abuse and eating disorders are at times the most difficult to deal with. The root problem is 'beliefs about who they are and how they think the world works.' People want to be happy, to belong, to be loved, and they also want to be competent in dealing with their lives.

Depression is also an area that Dr. Riches deals with on a regular basis. This is addressed by challenging beliefs, because the pain is not necessarily from a person's reality, but from what they believe about their reality. Depression causes chemical imbalance in the brain and this robs people of the ability to choose, and sometimes they choose 'death' by default. It is often misunderstood as sadness, but it's actually a lack of drive or energy and the ability to choose life.

People in the twentieth century often suffered from anxiety, but now in the twenty-first century, people suffer more from stress and depression. People who are perfectionists usually have irrational beliefs about themselves and situations, which therefore result in feelings of worthlessness and shame.

Effective treatment of depression is through these steps:

★ Diagnosis by a doctor, psychiatrist or psychologist
★ Medication (usually short-term)
★ Therapy (identifying self-destructive patterns and challenging irrational thinking regarding self-worth)
★ Positive thinking (personal responsibility)

Now, go and look into the mirror, love yourself and know your future is not determined by your past but decided by your actions today.

Be happy!

further reading

Dr. Dan B. Allender, *The Wounded Heart*, Crusade for World Revival (CWR), Surrey, UK, 1991.

Philip Baker, *Secrets of Super Achievers,* Webb & Partners, Perth, 1997.

Dr. Aaron T. Beck, *Love is Never Enough*, HarperCollins, New York, 1989.

Eileen Bradbury, *Counselling People with Disfigurement,* British Psychological Society, 1996.

Dr. Harriet B. Braiker, *The Disease to Please*, McGraw-Hill Books, New York, 2001.

Bob Burns & Tom Whiteman, *The Fresh Start Divorce Recovery Workbook*, Thomas Nelson Publishers, Tennessee, 1992.

Dr. Henry Cloud, *Changes That Heal,* Zondervan Publishing House, Michigan, 1993.

Dr. Henry Cloud & Dr. John Townsend, *Boundaries*, Zondervan Publishing
House, Michigan, 1992.

Gary Collins, *Counselling Families After Divorce,* Word Books, Texas, 1994.

Brangien Davis, *What's Real, What's Ideal: Overcoming a Negative Body Image*, The Rosen Publishing Group, New York, 1999.

Nancy Alcorn, *Mercy for Eating Disorders*, Providence House Publishers, Tennessee, 2003.

Dr. James Dobson, *Love Must Be Tough*, Word Books, Texas, 1983.

Douglas R. Flather, *The Resource Guide for Christian Counsellors*, Baker Books, Michigan, 1995.

Sarah Ford, *Teenagers Growing Up and Out*, *Sun-Herald*, Sydney, 5 October 1997.

Nancy Friday, *Jealousy*, M Evans & Co. Inc., New York, 1997.

Tim LaHaye & Bob Philips, *Anger is a Choice*, Zanderras, Michigan, 2002.

Gregory Landsman, *The Balance of Beauty*, Hill of Content Publishing Company, Melbourne, 1995.

Cathy Ann Matthews, *Breaking Through*, Albatross Books, Sydney, 1990.

Cynthia Rowland McClure, *The Monster Within*, Baker Book House Company, Michigan, 1984.

Dr. Phillip C McGraw, *Self Matters*, Simon & Schuster Source, New York,
2001.

Joyce Meyer, *The Root of Rejection*, Harrison House Publishers Oklahoma, 1995

M Gary Neuman & Patricia Romanowski, *Helping Your Kids Cope with Divorce the Sandcastles Way*, Random House, New York, 1998.

Merrell Noden, *Oprah Winfrey*, Time Inc., Bishop Books, New York, 1999.

Jessie H. O'Neill, *The Golden Ghetto: The Psychology of Affluence*, The
Affluenza Project, Milwaukee, Hazelden, 1996.

Dr. Mary Pipher, *Eating Disorders*, Vermilion Books, London, 1997.

Kay Marie Porterfield, *Violent Voices: 12 Steps to Freedom from Emotional and Verbal Abuse*, Health Communications, Florida, 1989.

Ayn Rand & Peter Schwartz, *Return of the Primitive: The Anti-Industrial Resolution*, Plume Books, USA, 1999.

Serious Issues in School Survey, The Age, Melbourne, 2 July 1999.

Charles R. Swindoll, *The Grace Awakening*, Word Publishing, Texas, 1996.

Joni Eareckson Tada, *Secret Strength*, Multnomah Press, Oregon, 1989.

Doreen Trust, *Overcoming Disfigurement,* Sterling Pub. Co., 1986.

Janine Turner, *Home is Where the Hurt is*, Thorsons Publishing Group, Northamptonshire, UK, 1989.

Teens and Social Media
Experts say kids are growing up with more anxiety and less self-esteem. Rachel Ehmke, Senior Writer Child Mind Institute, Nov 26, 2013

Dianne Wilson, *Back in Shape After Baby*, HarperCollins Publishers, Sydney, 2001.

Dianne Wilson, *Fat Free Forever!*, Random House Publishers, Sydney, 1996.

Dianne Wilson, *Easy Exercise for Everyone*, Random House Publishers, Sydney, 1997.

Dianne Wilson, *Fat Free Forever Cookbook,* Random House Publishers, Sydney, 1999.

Dianne Wilson, *Fat Free Forever 101 Tips*, Random House Publishers, Sydney, 1999.

Dianne Wilson, *Here to Eternity*, Harper Collins Publishers, Sydney, 2006.

Dianne Wilson, *Body & Soul*, USA, 2010, 2011